TALK OF THE DEVIL

Riccardo Orizio is the author of *Lost White Tribes*, which was shortlisted for the Thomas Cook Travel Book Award. He lives in Kenya.

ALSO BY RICCARDO ORIZIO

Lost White Tribes: Journeys Among the Forgotten

Riccardo Orizio

TALK OF THE DEVIL

Encounters with Seven Dictators

TRANSLATED FROM THE ITALIAN BY
Avril Bardoni

VINTAGE

321.90922/2016500

Published by Vintage 2004

2 4 6 8 10 9 7 5 3 1

Copyright © Riccardo Orizio 2002
Translation copyright © Avril Bardoni 2003

Riccardo Orizio has asserted his right under the Copyright,
Designs and Patents Act, 1988 to be identified as the author
of this work

First published in Great Britain in 2003 by
Secker & Warburg

Vintage
Random House, 20 Vauxhall Bridge Road,
London SW1V 2SA

Random House Australia (Pty) Limited
20 Alfred Street, Milsons Point, Sydney
New South Wales 2061, Australia

Random House New Zealand Limited
18 Poland Road, Glenfield,
Auckland 10, New Zealand

Random House (Pty) Limited
Endulini, 5A Jubilee Road, Parktown 2193,
South Africa

The Random House Group Limited Reg. No. 954009
www.randomhouse.co.uk

A CIP catalogue record for this book
is available from the British Library

ISBN 0 099 44067 9

Papers used by Random House are natural, recyclable
products made from wood grown in sustainable forests.
The manufacturing processes conform to the environ-
mental regulations of the country of origin

Printed and bound in Denmark by
Nørhaven Paperback, Viborg

Contents

For my father

For many years I kept two old, yellowing newspaper cuttings which, despite many a good resolution, I had never had the heart to throw away. When one wallet wore out, I transferred them to the new one. When they became creased, I pressed them between a banknote and a plastic phone-card.

For all their apparent flimsiness and fragility, they survived every kind of maltreatment. Over the years they fell out in the most diverse places: in the hallway of an Istanbul hotel at the feet of a *mafioso* wearing a purple shirt; at the check-in desk at Split airport; behind craters newly blasted out by Serb navy shells; at the home of an old school-friend in Brescia. I even remember them falling out as I searched for a business card before interviewing the republican leader Gerry Adams in a windowless room behind a steel door in the Falls Road in Belfast. Each time I was tempted to leave them lying on the floor, but each time I picked them up and replaced them in the wallet, giving them yet another lease of life.

Told like that, it might seem that the two cuttings lived a pretty exotic and adventurous life. In reality, most of the time they accompanied me to the newsroom of the paper in Milan where I worked as a journalist. They shared my long hours of boredom and frustration. Sometimes, during those late afternoon hours when the pages have yet to be composed and one is wondering how the paper is ever going to make the news-stands by the morning, I would take them out and look

I

at them. Occasionally even read them. In their own way, they kept my spirits up.

I had come by my two clippings while rummaging casually among the foreign newspapers finished with and waiting to be shredded. They were not the only clippings I kept, of course. I had whole piles of them, sorted by subject. Not the subjects I normally dealt with; rather those I dreamed of covering, but to which the editor never assigned me. I had a bulging folder dedicated to the Falklands. Another dealing with mercenaries fighting in various post-colonial wars. One file was devoted to the last white settlers in Sri Lanka. Others to obscure African countries such as Equatorial Guinea and Togo, theatres for whose tragedies the papers never found space. We all did the same. I remember a colleague who had a cupboard stuffed with material about certain Islamic terrorists of whom nobody, at the time, had ever heard. Another whose prize collection was in a file labelled 'Bulgaria'.

But my clippings were different. Together, they were my talisman. One day they might come in handy, I thought. Eventually they became part of me. Like the identity card that we Italians keep in our pockets.

I was struck by their similarity. Both referred to personalities accused of cannibalism. Both referred to former African dictators. Both had been clipped from the *Guardian*, a London newspaper that has always had its eye on the perversions of the world. One of the clippings was headlined 'Former Emperor Goes Home and Proclaims His Sainthood', the other 'Former Uganda Dictator Goes Shopping in the Frozen Food Aisle'. The former referred to Jean-Bedel Bokassa. The latter to Idi Amin.

Resigned to my paper's indifference to the Falklands and to Equatorial Guinea, I took out the two clippings one day and used them as a starting point for research into those fallen tyrants. I tracked down others, in many different countries and over several years, the search continuing even after I left the newspaper. Each personified an obscure, forgotten chapter of history. Some were willing to speak to me. Others agreed to speak but refused permission to quote them.

Valentine Strasser, one-time dictator of Sierra Leone, fell into the second category – although we drank many a bottle of Coca-Cola together at the table of a London hotel. Valentine was then thirty-five years old, tall and with the looks of a male model. He came to power with a coup d'état when only twenty-six, the youngest ever Commonwealth head of state. At summit meetings with fellow representatives of former British colonies, when the others went to bed, he slipped out to a disco. When Strasser (a former army captain) was driven out of power by another coup d'état after only five years, the British government procured him a place at Warwick University. Ironically, with a UN scholarship. But Strasser's academic aspirations were short-lived. He was forced out after being recognised by a fellow student from Sierra Leone, the daughter of a former minister he had sent to prison. She denounced him to the Students' Union – and the Students' Union demanded the immediate removal of an African tyrant from Warwick's so-immaculate halls of learning.

When I first met Strasser he was just one of many homeless Africans living in London. Sometimes he slept at the house of one of his girlfriends, at other times with some acquaintance from Sierra Leone. He often ended up in the home of a Sierra Leone Embassy official, still grateful for a foreign appointment made many years ago. When Strasser was president, Sierra Leone was flowing with blood, weapons and diamonds, but the handsome Valentine only had any truck with the first two. He never even had a bank account. His most prized possession was a Versace shirt in glittery material that made him look as if he was about to sally forth to the disco.

In May 2000 Valentine Strasser was beaten up in the street by several fellow countrymen, relatives of victims of his short and turbulent presidency. He fled from London with his face still bruised and swollen and applied for asylum to Guinea, which was governed by a man he believed to be his friend. It was refused. Eventually he went back to Freetown in Sierra Leone, where he lives with his mother and is harassed by passers-by when he dares to walk the streets.

Strasser is young and can, perhaps, rebuild his life. His ambition – at least when I last saw him – was to be a marketing manager. Perhaps the future will find him behind a desk in some office in Lagos or Lomé, anonymous and forgotten.

But what goes through the mind of someone who has had everything, lost everything and has no time to start again? How does a one-time dictator, whom the history books describe as ruthless, immoral and power-crazed, grow old? What does he tell his children and grandchildren about himself? What does he tell himself?

Sir Ian McKellen, who over an acting career spanning forty years has brought to life monsters of every epoch from Iago to Rasputin, has said, 'One of the few lessons I have learned from studying people who do terrible things is that they are all too human. And that we are all too capable of doing almost anything.'

The two yellowed clippings were my passport. And they led me, eventually, to Bokassa and Amin. I found the former in Bangui, the capital of the Central African Republic, living in one of his by now crumbling villas, dressed in the white robes of a holy man. He called himself an apostle of the Catholic Church. By an ironic coincidence, Idi Amin – when I finally tracked him down – was also dressed in white from head to foot. But the reason is that he is now living in Saudi Arabia and passes for a devout Muslim. Both impressed me as being sane and insane at one and the same time.

I encouraged them to voice their thoughts, these one-time tyrants. But I deliberately chose those who had fallen from power in disgrace, because those who fall on their feet tend not to examine their own conscience. Augusto Pinochet, for example, is still a powerful figure, revered by many in Chile. Suharto has been driven from power in Indonesia, but is protected by his wealth. Imelda Marcos, despite being indicted for corruption, has returned to Manila and amassed yet another huge collection of exclusive footwear. Alfredo Stroessner, the stereotypical Latin American dictator ousted from Paraguay in 1989, will always be guaranteed a safe haven in Brazil.

The tyrants in this book do not have the consolation of wealth, or if they live in comfort do not have that of immunity. Of the two cannibals of the clippings, the megalomaniac Bokassa died in poverty. Idi Amin enjoys perfect health, but the nearest he gets to luxury is a subscription to the gym of a hotel in Jeddah. Jean-Claude Duvalier was, for a period, too poor even to pay his household bills. Several, like Nexhmije Hoxha, have spent time in prison and now live very modestly. Others who fear the same fate are General Wojciech Jaruzelski, Mengistu Haile-Mariam and Mira Milosevic (whose husband and accomplice, Slobodan, is already behind bars). Sometimes they derive consolation from knowing that the countries from which they were forced to flee are now worse off than when they were in power.

The fallen dictators, it would seem, are not the cause of all the ills that befell their countries, but only of some. In their own eyes, sometimes not even that.

Wojciech Jaruzelski is in no doubt that Poland is indebted to him for having spared the country Soviet intervention by the introduction of martial law in December 1981. One who prefers to remain silent is Egon Krenz, the last East German head of state, the man who succeeded Erich Honecker before his world – the system, the Wall and Communism itself – collapsed. Sentenced to six and a half years in prison for ordering the shooting of refugees trying to cross into capitalist Berlin, he too will be young enough when freed to make something of his life. Like Jaruzelski, he suffers from a sense of injustice. 'They say I'm a murderer,' he told me. 'But I was a politician. I had my ideals. I believed in Socialism. If I am guilty, then so is a whole generation. Anyone in my position would have done the same.'

This reflection also sustains the other former tyrants. I do not

5

know whether or not it is true. I do not even know whether we can forgive them. We can only study them. And perhaps the exercise will help us to reach a greater understanding of ourselves.

Amin

A greying official in tails . . . sounded a gong and then, straightening up, read from a paper: 'His Excellency President for Life Field Marshal Al Hadj Doctor Idi Amin Dada, VC, DSO, MC, Lord of All the Beasts of the Earth and Fishes of the Sea and Conqueror of the British Empire in Africa in General and Uganda in Particular welcomes the Court of Kampala and assembled worthies of the city to this his annual banquet.

from *The Last King of Scotland* by Giles Foden

As one flies into Jeddah at dawn, the city looks as though someone has just thrown a bucket of whitewash over it.

The light is already dazzling, but the air is still cool. The huge airport appears deserted. The terminals open to the public – five or maybe ten of them, standing one behind the other – are empty. Those reserved for the royal family gleam in the desert, sealed and inaccessible. Rows of white condominiums built during the economic boom are separated by expanses of gelatinous sand. Mosques and supermarkets seem frozen in the surreal glacé icing, sticky and transparent, that overlays the Arabian desert in the passage between night and day.

As yet unbroken by the roar of air-conditioning, the silence of a Jeddah dawn is sinister.

I am in a car with my official escort, a functionary of the Ministry of Information, tall and mistrustful. He was waiting for me beside the steps of the aircraft when I arrived from Rome. Without even asking my name – as if he knew me already – he whisked me through passport control and customs

9

with a couple of brusque words to the officials. The driver is a foreigner, a black African. Not once has he met my eyes. Both are wearing the regular garb of the loyal Saudi subject: the long white robe called *thawb*, black Italian moccasins, and round the head the *ghutra an iqal,* a shawl secured with a black cord.

I feel uneasy. I have the sensation that Abdullah, my escort, is reading my mind, that he knows my secret. I try to distract him with preposterous questions about trade relations between our two countries and about the friendship uniting them. Then I pluck up the courage to ask him about the austerity measures recently adopted by the Saudi government, indeed by his own family, to control the unprecedented economic crisis. Abdullah replies in monosyllables. He loosens up only when revealing that he worked for a year in London, at the bureau of the Saudi news agency. 'As a journalist?' I ask. No. I try the alternative. 'Business manager?' Another negative. So I opt for silence. After a while he says, 'As an observer of English life.' Then, with evident sorrow, he adds, 'But the Ministry of Information withdrew the funding and I had to come home.'

Abdullah must be aware that I am the first Italian journalist in a long time to have been granted a visa. Sitting in the car, he regards me with curiosity. Perhaps he's wondering who my highly placed friends are. I would certainly not be here were it not for a recent and bizarre diplomatic initiative on the part of our minister for foreign affairs, who visited Saudi Arabia three times in less than twelve months. His first visit was seen in the light of a long-overdue repayment of a diplomatic debt. The two that followed shortly afterwards amazed even the Saudis, who called them 'an unequivocal demonstration of interest in us'. Absolutely true. For the most part, Western dignitaries like to make only brief and infrequent visits to the kingdom of Saudi Arabia, where the temperature is always too hot and the smiles too cold.

At the Saudi Embassy in London's Mayfair, a Fleet Street veteran who now has the job of spokesman had been perfectly frank: 'A visa? I can't remember the last time I signed one of these. I've got hundreds of requests sitting in a drawer. To be honest, I wouldn't get your hopes up.'

Many months later I managed to get an appointment at the Saudi Embassy in Rome, a nineteenth-century villa ruled over by a powerful prince of the royal family. In the guise of a rambling conversation about what I wanted to do in Saudi Arabia and why, I was subjected to a kind of 'test of trustworthiness'. In charge of this was a young diplomat who was noticeably uncertain about what to do with me. He spent much of the time taking calls on his mobile phone from friends and relatives all over the world and then apologising. 'That was my cousin so-and-so, calling from Toronto. Ah, that was my brother, from Abu Dhabi.'

We agreed on an itinerary starting in Jeddah, the financial capital of the country, then on to Jubail, an industrial complex in the desert consisting of a cluster of refineries and factories built by Filipino contract labour and considered a 'model city' by the Saudis, and finally to Riyadh. Times were fixed, appointments booked. Saudi Arabia, the young attaché said with an ironic smile, was always anxious that the foreign press should receive all possible assistance.

I passed the trustworthiness test. I told no lies, but had to conceal part of the truth. My paper, I explained, wanted interviews with Italian contractors doing business in Saudi Arabia, and articles about the development of the economy from oil-dependency to industrial diversification. All true. But I also had a secret agenda, one that would not pass any test.

In Jeddah my real objective was to find a man of seventy-two, height 1.96 metres, weight 150 kilos, long absent from the international stage he once dominated. A giant who boasted of having been a reluctant cannibal, complaining that human flesh was too salty. A head of state who sent telegrams to Queen Elizabeth addressing her as 'Liz' and inviting her to visit his country 'if she wanted to meet a real man'. Who announced the dispatch to Britain of a shipload of vegetables 'to alleviate your severe economic recession'. A president who ordered the decapitation of his opponents to be transmitted live on television, specifying that 'they must wear white to make it easy to see the blood'.

The man I had to find was Idi Amin Dada, the corporal who became Uganda's 'Big Daddy', the innocuous 'gentle giant' – as the European press referred to him when he first came to power – who became a monster.

Nowadays the Africans – Sudanese, Ugandans, Somalis, Nigerians – are leaving Jeddah. The exodus started at the end of the Nineties, when the economic crisis brought about by the collapse of oil prices forced the Saudi government to cut subsidies and apply immigration laws. Many Africans were literally rounded up in the streets and deported.

After the Africans, it was the turn of the Pakistanis, Bengalis and Indians.

The Africans who remain in the old kasbah struggle to keep their shops open, selling bogus perfumes, pastel-coloured shoes, soap, mirrors. Modest wares aimed at fellow immigrants whose numbers dwindle by the day.

The Saudis shop elsewhere, in malls which even at midnight are still crowded. These are the only public places that women are allowed to frequent. Veiled from head to foot, they walk around for hours in large groups, clutching the hands of their obese children. Their faces are invisible. Two holes for the eyes, one for the nose. On their hands they wear long black gloves similar to those that European women used to wear to the opera early in the twentieth century.

Giggling and whispering among themselves, the Saudi women buy, buy, buy, because there is nothing else to do. If they are caught speaking to a man who is not a relative, the special police patrols responsible for enforcing respect for Islamic customs can beat them with bamboo canes.

Jeddah has a beautiful sea front. By day it is deserted. Families have their picnics at night, when the heat is more bearable.

Arab music streams from car radios in the BMWs. Men sit cross-legged on the sand, smoking. Women and their children form separate groups. Boys kick a football around. Beach picnics help to maintain links with the nomadic traditions of grandparents who travelled the desert routes with their caravans.

Every evening, when Abdullah leaves me at my hotel after a day of meetings with bankers, businessmen and government functionaries, my search for Idi Amin begins. I take a taxi, ask to be driven to the kasbah and, passing en route the families intent on their sea-front picnics, begin to trawl through the African shops and stalls. The taxi driver is usually a sullen Saudi, with a ferocious grin revealing a mouthful of gold teeth, but one evening I happen to get an Indian. I ask him what his life is like in Saudi Arabia. He says, 'Fine.' Then adds, as if by way of illustration, 'There was a public execution today, in a square just near here. He was a foreigner, they say. Pakistani.'

In the kasbah I ask about Idi Amin. The name strikes a sympathetic chord with everyone, and they react as if talking about a relative who has made his fortune and moved to a trendier neighbourhood. 'We used to see him often here in the town centre, either before or after prayers in the mosque. It's a while now since I've seen him. I've heard he shops at one of the fashionable supermarkets. I can give you directions how to get there,' offers a Sudanese from behind a counter piled with bottles of shampoo.

I go to the supermarket. The cashiers are all Filipinos. The Saudis like them because they look submissive and all claim to come from the predominantly Muslim island of Mindanao. It's half-past eleven at night and families jostle in front of the food displays as if they were in Old Bond Street.

'Amin? Yes, he used to come here,' says a Filipino girl. And now? She shrugs her shoulders. 'He used to live in this part of town. Then, I suppose, he moved. He does his shopping somewhere else.'

The following day I have a stroke of luck. I encounter a

young Somali. Having made me promise not to get him into trouble, he tells me, 'Idi Amin used to be a boxer. He fought in the ring as a heavyweight before and after becoming president.' He's right. I remember reading about Amin's passion for boxing. In 1951, when he was a corporal in the army, he won the heavyweight title of Uganda and held it until 1960. Then he lost to an Italian stonemason called Serra, shorter than Amin but quicker on his feet. In 1971, by now elevated to the presidency after ousting Milton Obote with a military coup, his love of boxing resurfaced. Threatening to auto-select himself for the Ugandan Olympic team, he fought several of the contestants. All were soundly defeated.

'If you want to find him,' says the Somali reasonably, 'go to the gyms. There they know him well.'

The next day at my hotel they inform me that the best gyms and health centres all belong to their competitors, hotels such as the Intercontinental, Meridien, Sofitel. It's four o'clock in the afternoon and an already exhausted Abdullah asks if he may go home. I decide that it's time to visit the gyms.

At the last – a terrace with a swimming pool and a view over the nondescript boulevards of Jeddah – an Egyptian masseur opens his appointment book for me, placing it on a lectern like the Bible in church, and points to the name of Amin against a booking dated three months previously. 'That,' he says, 'was the last time I saw him.'

In the course of the next few days I get to know every masseur in Jeddah. And I start to reconstruct Amin's life. They tell me that he arrives in a white Range Rover. During the early years of his exile he drove a light-blue Cadillac. Then he acquired a Chevrolet Caprice. He has always liked cars. In Kampala he owned a red Maserati, and one of his little pleasures was to act as starter at the yearly rally across the savannah, then jump into his own sports car and chase after the competitors, all of whom politely – not to say wisely – allowed themselves to be overtaken.

In Jeddah he leaves whichever car he happens to be using at the time in the hands of the valet of the hotel where he has decided to start his day. He usually lunches at the Meridien, then goes to the Sofitel for tea. Or vice versa. For a swim or a massage he likes the Intercontinental. And his evening ends with coffee with his family at the Al Waha, a small hotel not very popular with foreigners.

He lives in reception halls. Like someone in transit. Perhaps deluding himself with the possibility of resuming his own journey. Or maybe a hotel is the only place where he can find someone to talk to during the day. Since 1980 Idi has officially had nothing to do except spend the salary bestowed upon him by the Saudi government in the name of 'Islamic solidarity'.

The Egyptian masseur and his colleague, the Intercontinental gym's resident trainer, remember Idi Amin's tips, and his laughter, with nostalgia. 'Complete nonsense, all that talk about crimes and murders,' they say with the confidence of men who have seen the world and massaged plenty of famous loins. 'It's the Americans, spreading lies as usual. From what we've seen, Idi Amin is a real gentleman who wouldn't hurt a fly. A great guy. As long as you don't ask him about his time as president. He doesn't like questions about the past. But when he comes here with his children he laughs and jokes with everyone.' And, as proof positive of moral integrity, they add, 'He swims to keep himself in shape, you know.'

Next day, as we enter the main hall of a bank dominated by portraits of the king and his heir, a gloomier-than-usual Abdullah asks, out of the blue, 'Tell me, what do you do in the evenings?'

I reply that I sometimes go out to sample the sights of the city. 'And,' I add, 'I go shopping.' This seems to satisfy him. However, he has some advice for me. 'Tomorrow is Friday. I suggest you stay in your hotel room. Or you could ask if anything has been organised for foreigners.'

✱ ✱ ✱

Something has. The receptionist who hands me my key announces, without waiting for any possible objection, 'You're all going to the beach tomorrow.' 'You' means the infidels, the foreigners. But what beach? Maybe it's the one stretch of desert where an acquaintance mentioned that bathing costumes are allowed, a beach reserved for non-Saudis. The coral reef, they say, is fantastic.

The following day an air-conditioned coach, transport for the infidels, draws up in front of my hotel. There is an entire Lufthansa crew on board, the women swathed in black veils from head to foot and wearing gloves. They laugh and tease each other in German. It's an enjoyable, even if enforced, day out. The fish in the sea are rainbow-coloured. A Lebanese family with the usual Filipino nanny plays Monopoly. The Germans keep themselves to themselves.

But I am impatient to resume the hunt. My time is running out. The next target is Hotel Al Waha. I look for the name in the guide handed out to foreigners, but it's not there. I ask at reception, but they don't know where it is. Eventually, after dark, a taxi driver locates it.

Sickly green lights. Piles of rubbish in the car park. The neon lights on the sign are half-blown. If you are looking for tranquillity, Al Waha has it in spades. Inside, the air is stale. Faded leather sofas. Gaudy Van Gogh reproductions on the walls. Two young men at the reception desk tell me to come back tomorrow. I dig my heels in. A voice comes from the manager's office. 'The boss says to go in,' they tell me.

The manager is an Indian with a beautifully trimmed moustache and a big ring on his finger. Proud of the certificates from hotel and catering colleges hanging behind his desk. 'Oh yes, I know everything about Idi Amin,' he announces. 'He is one of my best customers. A delightful man.'

Idi, the army cook who rose to the rank of general and eventually proclaimed himself 'the only president in direct contact with God', seems to have a soft spot for the unassuming Hotel Al Waha. I hear how he comes in, settles himself with his wife and children on the sofas, orders tea and cakes, invites other guests to join him, holds court.

'Every day, every single day,' says the manager, still incredulous. 'When he started coming here, after a while we became friends. He doesn't speak Arabic very well and with me he can talk freely in English. With great daring, I once asked him if the rumours were true, all those terrible stories . . . The murder of thousands of his opponents. The expulsion of thousands of Indian shopkeepers and their families . . . He gave a great shout of laughter and replied, "My friend, these were all lies invented to discredit me. The Americans and the English said I was mad because I wouldn't lick their boots. Do I look like a madman to you?"'

'How could anyone not believe him?' asks the Indian. He looks at me expectantly, waiting for my response. I can't think of one. He seems to appreciate my reticence. 'My friend, Saudi Arabia is a tricky place. Not everything is what it seems to be. People do not always speak the truth,' he adds, pleased with such a revelation.

What is he trying to say? The Indian glances over his shoulder. He speaks as if the walls of the Al Waha (much in need of a coat of paint) are hiding a host of spicy secrets. 'Take the women. Veiled, unapproachable, right? Yet I, with my own eyes, have seen a princess of the royal family take off her clothes in front of a group of men and invite them to . . .' He stops himself. 'Beautiful girl. When she took off her veil, underneath she was dressed like a European woman. Very stylish.'

And what happened next?

The manager shakes his head, mumbling, 'I can't, I can't', and quickly returns to the subject of Idi Amin. 'I've got Idi's home telephone number and his address. Strangely enough, I haven't seen him for a while. Give me time to make a few enquiries and I'll be able to tell you where he is. We foreigners must help each other, right?'

Word must have got around the hotel that I've been asking questions. One day, while waiting for a taxi, I get into conversation with a porter. He says, with a wink, 'I come from Uganda.' And waits. I pretend not to understand. I ask him about his family, about life as a foreigner. He's not interested in small talk. So I get down to brass tacks. 'How can I find Idi Amin?'

The porter is ready with his reply. 'One of his former ministers of justice used to work here in the hotel, in the accounts department. He's got his own business now.' I'd like to contact him, I say. The boy looks at me as if I had just asked for an audience with the king. 'He's busy. I'll try to have a word with him myself. He doesn't like strangers. But Idi and I are bosom pals.' Big Daddy can't give me the slip now, I think. And I relax.

Feeling confident about my manhunt, I realise that I've been neglecting my fellow countrymen and decide it's about time to call on them. There is still a large number of Italians in Jeddah where, in the Seventies and Eighties, they formed one of the biggest foreign communities. They were building roads and houses, as they have done the world over since the days of the Roman Empire. Here there was a desert to fill and unlimited state treasuries to empty. Both these factors now belong to the past. But the Italians have stayed. At the consul's residence one of them, for decades the Jeddah representative of a big shipping company, gives me some welcome information: only a few months ago he had been on the very brink of entering into a business deal with my man, Idi Amin Dada.

'One day he came into the office, jovial, self-confident, asked to speak to me and questioned me about the possibility of shipping some containers for him as a matter of urgency. A very ordinary sort of conversation. Then I recognised him, called him by his name, Mr Amin, and asked where he wanted them sent, these containers. He replied, 'Northern Uganda, near the Sudanese border. It's sensitive material, you understand. Important cargo.' The Italian mops his bald head. The mere thought of the peril so narrowly avoided – African plots involving war and guerrilla activities, illicit trafficking – was bringing him out in a sweat. 'I told him I was sorry, but we had no shipboard space available for the foreseeable future.'

So Idi Amin's attention is not focused exclusively on swimming pools and gyms. He has not taken to his rocking-chair just yet. Northern Uganda is his birthplace, but it is also the region where the government troops of President Yoweri Museveni are engaged in an endless conflict with guerrillas backed by the Islamic government of Sudan. Maybe, with Saudi approval, he's helping the Muslim guerrillas, hoping that this move will pave the way for his return to Kampala.

Maybe this plan has been part of his agenda since the beginning of his exile, in 1979. One day in June 1981, for example, he made an unexpected call from a public phone-box to the London *Guardian* (asking to be called back when he ran out of small change), declaring, in his halting English, 'I am telling you in advance that troops loyal to me are in the process of retaking Kampala under the leadership of Commander Nine-Nine.'

The mysterious Commander Nine-Nine never showed up in the city. But twenty years later it is possible that Idi Amin is still trying.

That he should turn to the Italians in a moment of need is not surprising. It is said in Jeddah that the aircraft which flew him in 1980 to Saudi Arabia from Tripoli, where Colonel Gaddafi had offered him temporary asylum after his flight from Kampala, sported the livery of Alitalia. The plane stood abandoned on the tarmac of the old Jeddah airport for years afterwards. Alitalia never reclaimed it. Perhaps it belonged to the pro-Libya wing of the Italian secret services. Offering Idi a lift could have been Italy's way of repaying an old debt to Gaddafi, impatient to be rid of this troublesome fellow Muslim.

As soon as he arrived in Jeddah, the Riyadh government put out a communiqué explaining that President Amin was visiting the kingdom 'on an extended pilgrimage'. King Fahd – who had financed the building of several mosques in Uganda and visited the country in person during Amin's presidency – had kept his promise of help in time of need.

That pilgrimage continues yet. Idi Amin is revered and respected for his piety. Abdul, a young pharmacist from Sudan, explains, 'He may have massacred thousands of people and even eaten the flesh of his enemies, but there comes a time when it is right to forgive. After all, he's not the only person in Africa to have done such things . . .'

Quite true. But Idi Amin Dada is the only one to have done these things with such farcical enthusiasm, with such a knack for the theatrical that it came very close to political satire.

On 19 July 1975, for instance, Idi had himself photographed sitting in a sedan chair borne by four skinny English businessmen, under the gaze of foreign ministers from member states of the Organisation for African Unity. A fifth white man, a Swede, marched behind him carrying a sunshade to protect the presidential head from the burning rays of the sun. A perfect parody of colonial daguerreotypes. The following day, in the presence of the same dignitaries, he re-celebrated his marriages to his wives (of which there were then three), insisting on wedding presents as his due.

He loved to humiliate people in public. Some time later he invited a crew of French cameramen to film a government meeting. In front of his terrorised ministers, Idi Amin launched a long, rambling monologue like a corporal drilling young and undisciplined recruits. The political highlight of the meeting was the famous threat: 'The third consecutive time that I call a minister and I don't find him in his office – because they tell me he is out, tending his business or something like that – he's fired. Including the foreign minister.' And a camera catches the wretched man, his head buried in the papers he is carrying, all too aware of the tragic destiny that awaits him.

Idi never lost his appetite for cruel farce. In the course of a television programme he sacked his new foreign minister for nothing more nor less than sexual misbehaviour. Protagonist of this affair was the splendid Princess Elizabeth Bagaya, daughter of the king of the Toro people (one of the main tribes in Uganda). The first Ugandan woman with a degree in law, the first to graduate from Oxford and the first to practise law in London, she was also an actress and modelled for *Vogue* magazine. For a while Elizabeth was the constant companion of Idi (who at the time already had four wives, three of whom he divorced without warning during another TV speech). No one has ever forgotten the time she kissed him in public, at the end of a famous boxing match in Kampala. It was a highly symbolic moment. Here was the illiterate but muscular boy from the countryside being kissed by the elegant, aristocratic beauty. It was as if the whole of Uganda – the gentle and attractive 'pearl of the British Empire' – had accepted him. A grateful Idi appointed Princess Elizabeth ambassador to Paris. Then ambassador to the United Nations. Then foreign minister in place of the unfortunate Michael Ondaga, whose public scolding had been seen in the French documentary. At this point Idi boasted – to his personal physician, a young Scotsman – of having eaten Ondaga's flesh, but this was just Idi's idea of a good joke. Ondaga was in fact simply found, dead, among the crocodiles of Lake Victoria.

For a while the risk of Elizabeth's sharing the fate of her predecessor seemed unlikely. But a few months after appointing her to the post, Idi Amin appeared on television in a rage. 'Our foreign minister,' he fulminated, 'has brought disgrace upon our nation by making love with a white man in a toilet at the Paris airport. She is dismissed.' Elizabeth fled to Kenya, where she accepted the hospitality of another Big Daddy, Jomo Kenyatta.

The princess got her own back eventually, putting her degrees and her beauty at the disposal of anti-Amin guerrillas and becoming their spokeswoman in Europe. As soon as Yoweri Museveni became president, he appointed her ambassador to Washington. She now practises law in Kampala and leads one faction of the fractious Toro royal family. Reluctant to speak about the past, she limits herself to saying, 'Idi Amin was mad, and I always knew it.'

One of the finance ministers was luckier. He misguidedly informed the president that the government coffers were empty. Idi Amin, a true African Caligula, exploded. 'Why you ministers always come nagging to President Amin? You are stupid. If we have no money, the solution is very simple: you should print new money.' The minister bowed, left the room and fled to London, thereby saving his skin.

Nobody could accuse Idi of being hypocritical. When accused of corruption, far from denying it, he replied, 'Running a country is like running a big business: you have to award yourself a decent salary!'

But Idi Amin's real passion was for international diplomacy. On Radio Kampala he once declared, 'Henry Kissinger is apparently not a very intelligent man. He never comes to Kampala to consult me about international affairs.'

His adoptive country was Scotland. In the Fifties Amin had been a soldier in a Scottish regiment stationed in colonial Kenya. The Scottish officers loved his physical energy and his loud laughter. And in return he loved their mockery of the English. Once he became president, he was tempted to follow the example of his fellow dictator, Jean-Bedel Bokassa of Central Africa, and proclaim himself Emperor of Uganda. But he eventually opted for the title of 'the last king of Scotland', and decreed that the Ugandan presidential guard should wear kilts and play bagpipes to signal support for Scottish separatism.

Perhaps involuntarily, he became a master of paradox. A few hours before an audience with Pope Paul VI, Idi Amin arrived at the Vatican in a uniform massively weighed down by bogus decorations 'awarded' by non-existent orders of chivalry, their names invented in a deliberate parody of those of imperial Britain. A political gesture? The Vatican of those days was still a very formal place, with aristocrats in full dress uniform and courtiers with strange and elaborate titles. So, afraid that Amin was engaging in parody, the pallid monsignors in charge of protocol persuaded him, though only at the last moment, to change into the more sober garb of a dark suit. Leaving Rome, he visited the Augusta helicopter factory, where he spent tens of millions of dollars on military machines. He ended his Italian tour in Milan, at the trade fair, where he shocked the assembled journalists by telling them, 'I'm here to promote tourism in Uganda, my beautiful country. I personally invite all the Italians to come to Uganda and freely shoot any elephant and rhinoceros they want.'

His first state visit to London, in July 1971, was even more bizarre. To begin with, Idi Amin arrived totally unexpectedly. He installed himself and his retinue in an hotel; the following day – as protocol required – he was invited to lunch with the queen, the prime minister Edward Heath and the foreign minister Sir Alec Douglas-Home. Over coffee the queen finally asked him, 'Tell me, Mr President, to what do we owe the unexpected pleasure of your visit?' The answer came unhesitatingly. 'I just needed to do some shopping. In Uganda, Your Majesty, it is difficult to find a pair of size-fourteen shoes.' The queen chose to regard this as a witticism.

Someone, however, made him understand that state visits require notice. So in February 1975 Radio Kampala claimed that Buckingham Palace had received the following letter from Idi Amin:

My dear Queen,

I intend to arrive in London for an official visit on August 4th this year, but I am writing now to give you time to make all the necessary preparations for my stay so that nothing important is omitted. I am particularly concerned about food, because I know that you are in the middle of a fearsome economic crisis. I would also like you to arrange for me to visit Scotland, Ireland and Wales to meet the heads of revolutionary movements fighting against your imperialist oppression.

Years later, when celebrations were afoot for the twenty-fifth anniversary of the queen's accession, Idi Amin announced that a 'friendly nation' – possibly Libya – had lent him a plane with which he planned to deliver 'a nice surprise'. In London there were rumours that Amin intended to descend upon the royal procession by parachute. The RAF was alerted to keep watch on the skies.

When not on official or state visits, Idi loved writing telegrams. Many of them have entered the annals of diplomatic history.

To Richard Nixon during the Watergate crisis: 'If your country does not understand you, come to Papa Amin who loves you. A kiss on both your cheeks.' And, as a postscript, a piece of advice: 'When the stability of a nation is in danger, the only solution is, unfortunately, to imprison the leaders of the opposition.'

To Leonid Brezhnev and Mao Tse-tung: 'Lately I have been thinking much about the Soviet Union and China. I am worried about them. I would like to see you happy. Your relations are not friendly. If you need a mediator I am at your disposal.'

To the Israeli government during the Yom Kippur war: 'I command you to surrender.'

To Kurt Waldheim, secretary-general of the United Nations (and a former Wehrmacht officer): 'I express my support for the historical figure of Adolf Hitler, who made war in order to unify Europe and whose only mistake was to lose it.' A few hours before this telegram was sent, Radio Kampala broadcast a statement by Field Marshal Idi Amin announcing the imminent construction of a statue dedicated to Hitler.

To the general secretary of the British Commonwealth: 'In view of the success of the economic revolution in Uganda, I maintain that I am the ideal candidate to lead the Commonwealth instead of Great Britain, which is suffering a serious economic crisis.'

To the Turkish government immediately after the invasion of Cyprus: 'I request to see your military plans and film footage of the landing because these will be useful to me the day my army attacks South Africa.'

★   ★   ★

24

Military exercises in preparation for the attack on South Africa included Field Marshal Amin christening an island facing his own villa on Lake Victoria 'Capetown' and having it constantly bombed by the air force. Also in the name of preparatory exercises, he gave the command to invade Tanzania. This was fatal. The Tanzanian leader Julius Nyerere, a heavyweight Marxist intellectual of diminutive physical stature whom Amin had once challenged to a boxing match, decided to put Idi on the canvas once and for all.

But in April 1979, as it happened, a private plane sent by Gaddafi saved Idi Amin from being lynched by the Tanzanian army and Ugandan rebels. The Libyan leader, who had persuaded Amin to break off diplomatic relations with Israel and side with the Arab terrorist organisations in exchange for economic aid, offered him the use of a villa on the Tripoli coast. Later Gaddafi sent him to the Saudis.

In Kampala, meanwhile, proof was emerging that behind the carnival antics of 'Big Daddy' there was a reeking trail of blood. The decapitated heads of some of his adversaries were discovered in the fridges of the presidential residence. On the hill of Nakasero, beside one of his villas, an extermination camp was found where emaciated prisoners survived by gnawing the bones of those already dead. Amin's closest adviser, an Englishman known as 'Major Bob', or 'the second most hated man in Uganda', was sent to prison accused of having run the 'State Research Bureau', the secret service responsible for the massacre of thousands. There were victims within Amin's own family, too. When his wife Kay, cousin of the unfortunate Ondaga, died, her arms and legs were cut off by order of the dictator because she had had an abortion. He then had the limbs sewn back, right to left and vice versa, and showed her to several of his relatives saying, 'Now you see what happens to wicked mothers.'

The country's economy was by now in ruins, in spite of – or perhaps even because of – the 'economic war' declared by Idi Amin. In 1972, 80,000 Indians were expelled from Uganda from one day to the next because he had had a dream, he said, in which 'God told me to do it'. Rumour had it that 'Big Daddy' was cross with the Asians because their most prominent family, the Madhvanis, a dynasty with substantial investments in Africa, had refused to give him the prettiest of their daughters as wife.

Even the Anglican archbishop of Kampala had been tortured and killed. The state radio spoke of a 'car accident'. His car had been riddled with bullets.

With Israel, Idi Amin had a strange love-hate relationship. As a promising young officer he had attended military training in Tel Aviv and while there had had treatment for syphilis; he was aware of a tribe in Uganda that had converted to Judaism, but chose Islam and expelled all the Israelis, calling them 'criminals'. So nobody was surprised when details emerged of what had gone on behind the scenes during the Entebbe hijacking saga. In 1976 a group of Palestinians hijacked an Air France plane carrying a hundred or so Israelis. Idi Amin allowed them to use the airport, but soldiers sent by Israel liberated all the hostages apart from one, a certain Dora Bloch, who had been wounded and consequently sent to Kampala hospital. Dora Bloch never went home: she became another victim of a 'car accident'.

In total, no fewer than 300,000 people were murdered while Idi Amin was in power.

One day in Jeddah I try to phone the Indian manager of the Hotel Al Waha, who has promised to help me, but he is never in his office. The former Ugandan minister has gone to ground, too. The porter has given me Amin's phone number, but no one ever answers. 'He must be on holiday,' says the porter. On holiday? But where? He doesn't know. In compensation, he has a suggestion to make. 'You know where you should go, where you'd be most likely to find President Amin?' No, I reply. That's why I'm trying to find the minister. He looks at me wide-eyed, amazed that I should be ignorant about something so simple.

'Idi Amin spends hours at the airport. That's where you should go.' The idea strikes me as bizarre. Is he trying to escape? No. The one-time field marshal now personally supervises the clearance through customs of food sent by his relatives in northern Uganda.

The well-informed porter lists the groceries shipped to Idi Amin with the precision of a cook restocking the larder on a morning visit to the market: the delicious hand-milled flour from the city of Koboko; the green bananas called matooke from the city of Masaka; cassava and millet from a favourite shop in Kampala. And this well-informed porter concludes, 'The president loves roast goat with cassava and millet. Can eat any amount of it.'

At the airport they corroborate the information. Yes, Amin is often here, but no one has seen him today. No bananas are due to be shipped in. My heart sinks.

One of Idi Amin's sons plays basketball at a Boston college. Two more run the Ugandan basketball federation. His wife Madina has returned to Kampala and President Museveni has returned her houses and land. Another son produces Uganda's most famous and irreverent radio programme, *The Capital Gang*, on Capital Radio. He could have been arrested and tortured for this during his father's regime. As for Idi Amin, his pardon is possibly not far away. Chapaa Karuhanga, leader of the opposition party, the National Democratic Forum, wants to pardon him 'in the name of national reconciliation'. And there is another reason. 'While they're in exile Amin and Obote are supporting the civil wars that are tearing this country apart. If we get them back it will be easier to control them.'

The reference to the support of civil wars is a reference to Idi's son, Taban Amin, nicknamed 'Sheriff'. He has been living for many years in the Congo (Zaire until 1997), at the fulcrum of all African wars, where he leads a small army of mercenaries. It fights wherever it can rattle the Ugandan army, which virtually controls the eastern region. Formerly, when

Uganda was supporting Joseph Kabila and opposing Mobutu, Amin's son fought with Mobutu, his father's friend. Then, when Kabila came to power in the Congo and broke with Uganda, 'Sheriff' Taban Amin changed sides and started to support the Kabila-led government.

In October 1998 Sheriff Taban Amin had to surrender the garrison at Kindu, one of the few still in the hands of the Kinshasa government. The Ugandans wiped it out. This seething snake-pit lies between the Kivu province of eastern Congo, southern Sudan and northern Uganda, where Africa's 'first world war' – as diplomats call it – has been fought for years.

Taban Amin retreated to Mbandaka, another garrison lost in the forests. His command is an unholy alliance of Sudanese tribal militiamen (Islamic Sudan hates Uganda) and former Hutu soldiers responsible for the genocide of the Tutsi in Rwanda. His other ally is a mysterious rebel army, the West Nile Bank Front, led by Amin's one-time foreign minister Juma Oris. Now realisation dawns. It was Taban to whom Amin had been planning to send the containers aboard the Italian ship. And they would not have been filled with green bananas.

I am about to leave Jeddah on my way to visit the refineries at Jubail. My escort Abdullah has disappeared. I go to say goodbye to the Ugandan hotel boy. 'You're going already?' he asks. 'Just when we've found the president?' 'We?' 'Me and my father, the ex-minister.'

The boy's face registers stupefaction at my not having made the connection. 'Idi Amin has gone to stay in Mecca for a while, at a house belonging to the royal family.'

Mecca is a city that infidels may not enter. They are either keeping Amin away from me or from ships bound for Africa. My hunt is over. Big Daddy has won.

'Don't worry, I've got his phone number. Let's go and give him a call,' says the porter.

Two hours later I'm on the phone in a phone-box. Idi Amin's powerful voice greets me with a laugh. 'I knew you were looking for me, but first I had to make sure you were not a spy. What do you want to know? I'm no longer interested in politics.'

What is your life here like, Mr President?

'Fine, absolutely fine. I'm a good Muslim and nowadays my only interests have to do with Islam. My sons are all grown up now and have left Jeddah. I have just sent two of them off to college in the United States. I've got a little daughter, Iman, and a young wife, but I am dedicated to religion and nothing else. I recite the Koran, play the organ, go swimming and fishing at a resort near the Yemeni border. The fish there are delicious, believe me. A peaceful life.'

What do you miss, Mr President?

'I miss Ugandan food. I miss my many friends. When I was president I used to go out in the evening with my friends, former boxing partners or the lads from the national football team. I loved to go dancing like an ordinary person. I'm first and foremost a boxing champion, as you know. An athlete.'

Do you keep abreast of events in politics? Are you still critical of Britain and the United States?

'That's history, that is all in the past. I keep up with international news, but I don't want to be mixed up in the affairs of the superpowers. At home in Jeddah I've got five satellite dishes, state-of-the-art. I watch television from all over the world. I speak many languages, including Lingala, the language of the Congo, where as a young officer I commanded a pro-Mobutu contingent. I must go now. The government doesn't want me to speak to the press. I'm only a guest here.'

And what have you got to say about the Uganda of today? And about Museveni?

'That he must stop discrediting me. I could call on almighty God and pray that something bad happens to him. And I hope that he will stop attacking the Congo, getting Africans to kill Africans.'

Do you feel any remorse?

'No. Only nostalgia.'

For what?

'For when I was a non-commissioned officer fighting against the Mau Mau in Kenya and everyone respected me. I was as strong as a bull. I was a good soldier in the British army. The terror of the Mau Mau. I was born in a very, very poor family. And I enlisted to escape hunger. But my officers were Scottish and they loved me. The Scots are good, you know.'

There is an old Manhattan Transfer song by Slinger Francisco called 'Wanted: dead or alive'. It goes:

> The rule of the tyrants decline
> The year, 1979
> From Uganda to Nicaragua
> It's bombs and bullets all the time
> So they corrupt, so they vile
> So it's coup after coup all the while
> Human rights they violate
> They think they too damn great
> So in disgrace now they live in exile.
>
> Gairy is a wanted man
> Idi Amin is a wanted man
> Shah of Iran tried so hard to survive
> He too was wanted dead or alive.

On my return to Jeddah a week later the porter greets me with a big smile. 'President Amin is in town, but not for long. He may be able to see you this evening. I'll take you there.'

Big Daddy is waiting for me on the second floor of a white villa surrounded by other white villas. A giant of a man, he is wearing a white cotton tunic and a skullcap. The protruding eyes, which seemed to jump out of the photographs showing him in braided uniforms, are unchanged. But Idi Amin Dada, self-appointed conqueror of the British Empire, only wants to show me his latest toy, satellite TV. His hands are trembling with excitement. His famous voice is as deep as it was twenty years ago, when he was spending his presidential days in fatigues staging fake invasions of Israel, so-called 'military exercises' intended to impress and ingratiate himself with the Islamic world.

'I wanted to prove to you that, *inshallah*' – he raises his eyes to the sky in accordance with Islamic law – 'I do not live cut off from the world, as they write in the Ugandan papers. I still have many friends. I follow all the news. I'm still a man of the world.'

The screen is as vast as Idi Amin himself. The former corporal runs through the channels, pressing the buttons on the remote control with a kind of quiet madness: BBC, Libyan TV, Saudi TV. He reels them off as if they were verses from the Koran.

Then he apologises. He has to leave. 'An urgent appointment,' he says. 'Perhaps we can speak next time you come to Jeddah.'

The hotel porter signals that I have to go. I see a white Cadillac leaving the garage. From another room comes the cry of a baby.

Manhattan Transfer were wrong. Idi Amin is 'a wanted man'. But Big Daddy does not find it 'hard to survive'.

He has long survived his alter ego, the other humble African soldier who rose through the colonial ranks to become president and dictator of his country: Jean-Bedel Bokassa of Central Africa. Both accused of cannibalism, both converted to Islam in order to please Colonel Gaddafi and receive his petro-dollars, Bokassa and Amin were too similar to become friends. They rarely met. But history dictated that their empires of terror would end in the same year: 1979. And in the same way: with military action on the part of a foreign power, France in the case of Bokassa and Tanzania in the case of Idi Amin.

They both had a taste for women, bogus decorations and army life. And maybe human flesh. They both fled in 1979, the same year that the Shah of Persia also fled Teheran. It was a bad year for tyrants. But the former corporal has never been prosecuted and jailed like Bokassa. In 1980, when Bokassa was sentenced to death *in absentia*, Idi Amin arrived safely in Jeddah and was welcomed by prominent members of the Saudi royal family. Unlike the former French officer who turned against his former colonial masters, the Big Daddy of Kampala found, on the day he fell, a Bigger Daddy to look after him.

The old boxer fell, but there was no KO.

He died in 2003 in a state-of-the-art Saudi hospital. In Uganda some asked the government to allow a burial in his hometown. Many obituaries around the world were full of nostalgia for the good old days when we all believed that Africa's only problem was a handful of mad dictators.

Bokassa

It was hard to believe that the ogre had undergone a genuine conversion, but unusual things happen when your fortune changes.

from *Nomad* by Mary Anne Fitzgerald

Leaning against a white wall at the far end of the room were the last remaining relics of his empire: a gilded throne upholstered in red velvet and a suit of armour. 'See that?' he asked me, pointing with his ivory-tipped cane without rising from the sofa. The cane was the same famous '*canne de justice*' that he had used in 1977 to beat the English reporter Michael Goldsmith. 'That suit of armour, it's medieval. It comes from Spain. General Franco's gift for my coronation. That day all the world's most powerful people had to come to Bangui. For the first time they bowed to an African emperor. Oh yes,' he added with a rapt expression on his face, 'right here in Bangui. And each one had to bring me a magnificent present.'

He stopped and looked at me, his eyes shining like those of a child on a birthday morning. I kept my head down and pretended to be taking notes. Although disappointed by my unwillingness to share his delight, Jean-Bedel Bokassa continued, 'That day I ceased to be the one who always had to give presents – diamonds, ivory, women . . . The international leaders respected me because I was an emperor.' And once again he pointed the ivory tip of the cane at the suit of armour. As if the ancient relic contained – besides a handful of African insects baked to a frazzle by the heat – proof of his imperial dignity.

★   ★   ★

35

But the most bizarre ceremony of recent history had not gone quite as Bokassa remembered it.

On that remarkable day, 4 December 1977, in the Palais des Sports Jean-Bedel Bokassa, on Bokassa Avenue, next to the Jean-Bedel Bokassa University, the absentees had been more notable than the attendees. And the coronation had not been the first where the 'civilised world' had bowed to an African emperor.

For Haile Selassie's coronation in 1930, when the celebrations had lasted three days in the steamy hills of Addis Ababa, all the great powers had sent high-level delegations or members of their respective royal families, despite the discomforts of the journey. The Duke of Gloucester, brother of Edward VIII and George VI, travelled from London. Prince Eugenio di Savoia came from Rome. Plenipotentiaries were even sent from Moscow and Washington.

The coronation of Bokassa the First was, by contrast, snubbed even by his fellow autocrats. General Franco stayed away. The Spanish suit of armour travelled alone, on a ship. Emperor Hirohito of Japan and Shah Reza Pahlavi of Iran, the first to be invited because Bokassa considered them his only equals in rank, made their excuses. Haile Selassie's prestigious name did not figure on the guest list because he had been dead for two years, probably strangled by a young army officer whose name – Mengistu Haile-Mariam – was going to become notorious well beyond Ethiopia. Of the 500 foreign dignitaries present, the most prominent were a relative of the prince of Liechtenstein, Count Emmanuel, and the prime minister of Mauritius, Sir Seewoosagur Ramgoolam. Not even Idi Amin of Uganda, Mobutu Sese Seko of Zaire or Omar Bongo of Gabon, old African friends of Bokassa's and fellow autocrats, cared to compromise themselves. Idi Amin declined the invitation on the grounds that he would risk being kidnapped by Israeli paratroopers as a consequence of the Entebbe blitz, and, besides, he was busy with his plans to invade white-ruled South Africa.

Many of the 'magnificent presents' – possibly even the Spanish suit of armour – revealed themselves on close inspection to be worthless. Only France had been truly generous (and one day the world would learn the reason why). The government in Paris 'lent' the twenty-two million dollars Bokassa needed to buy ceremonial dress for thousands of guests, a throne in the form of a Napoleonic eagle three and a half metres high and five wide, a gilded imperial carriage with eight white Belgian-schooled horses, a crown by the Parisian jeweller Arthus Bertrand containing diamonds, some of which were as big as eighty carats, two official portraits by the German artist Hans Linus, and music (an imperial march and imperial waltz) commissioned from a French composer. Plus 24,000 bottles of Moët et Chandon and 4,000 bottles of Château Mouton-Rothschild and Château Lafite-Rothschild. Plus sixty Mercedes cars shipped from Germany to the Cameroons and then flown over the forest to Bangui. Not to forget the troop of mounted 'Hussars' formed and kitted out in nineteenth-century-style brocade uniforms expressly for the occasion, who escorted the imperial carriage.

Bokassa's eyes lit up as he listened to the catalogue of preposterous European luxuries jetted into the heart of Africa, luxuries never before seen in Bangui, a town still permeated with the smoky smell of an African village, lying sleepily on the banks of a muddy river heaving with hippopotamus.

'All true. But is there anything wrong with that?' he asked. His flat voice had acquired a hard edge. His grasp tightened on the cane. 'It was the least the French could do to repay me for my services as a soldier fighting for their country, and for all the personal favours their politicians received when I became president. I am the son of a king. I always knew that one day I would be crowned with great celebration. My coronation was organised to give dignity to my country in the eyes of the rest of the world. The Central African government did not incur the debt of a single franc for the coronation. I did what any other African king would have done. And if Mobutu and Idi Amin chose not to come, it was because they were jealous of my becoming emperor. Jealous of my idea.'

He fell suddenly silent. His eyelids drooped. It looked as if he had fallen asleep. A man improbably attired in a tailcoat was tiptoeing across the big room towards Bokassa's sofa, where the emperor was protected by a white curtain from the blazing sun of the Central African Republic. He trod warily on the rotten ceramic tiles, grimacing every time one wobbled and grated against its neighbour.

'My cabinet secretary,' the one-time emperor explained, jabbing the cane in his direction with less enthusiasm than he had jabbed at the suit of armour. The courtier assented solemnly, head bowed.

Bokassa launched into one of his countless tirades against the French. He had done this already two or three times in the few hours we had spent together. He listed his grievances in a flat monotone, like a lawyer reading a will when the contents are already known to all members of the family of the deceased.

First, the volte-face of the once-loved adoptive country, the country for which he had fought in three continents and which had then robbed him of his castles, crown and reputation. Then the 'betrayal' by Valéry Giscard d'Estaing, once his 'dear cousin', avid hunter of elephants and women, who was behind his removal from power. Then there was the sexual infidelity of the Empress Catherine, accused of being Giscard's mistress and of having shared with him the treasures termed by Bokassa, in a moment of rare sincerity, 'my Aladdin's cave'.

'I even fought for France in Indo-China, after enrolling here in Africa. Oh yes, Indo-China. I fought against the Nazis with the forces of the Free French. I sacrificed my youth to France. And that despite the fact that the French had killed my father before my very eyes, right in front of M'Baiki's police headquarters. My father was a chief who opposed the colonial occupation. My mother killed herself shortly afterwards, in desperation. I was six years old. And yet I fought for France for twenty-two years. They decorated me, giving me the Croix

38

de Guerre, two Croix de la Résistance, the Légion d'honneur and an officer's pension. When they wanted diamonds, the politicians in Paris hinted at a second Croix de Guerre. And I didn't give the diamonds only to Giscard. I gave them to many people, in France and other places. The only reason I won't mention names is because . . . because I don't want to make more enemies. But I'm so anti-French now that if I still had those decorations, I'd throw them in a dustbin in front of the television cameras.'

The cabinet secretary began to laugh, a loud, forced laugh. Meanwhile he had, with great deliberation, pushed a china tray laden with medicines towards Bokassa. There were phials, rectangular boxes, little bottles with French labels. The emperor pretended not to notice. But the man in tails refused to admit defeat. Bokassa looked at the tray with disgust. 'I'm very ill, it's difficult for me to move now. I can't stand on my feet for more than two minutes – no, two seconds. The French have tried to poison me on several occasions. They did poison me. They have poisoned me.'

The African gentleman nodded, his head still bowed, while continuing to nudge the tray nearer to Bokassa. 'But I survived. No thanks to the medicines, but thanks to this.' And he was suddenly brandishing the heavy silver cross that until that moment had stood on the coffee table in front of the sofa. It was a piece of sculpture half a metre high, a solid cross standing on alpine rocks with an emaciated Christ at the centre. 'Paul VI gave it to me when he secretly nominated me thirteenth apostle of Holy Mother Church.'

I looked up from my notebook. Perhaps I hadn't understood properly.

The one-time emperor was indeed dressed all in white, in a priestly robe that reached right down to his rubber flip-flops. Another crucifix hung on a chain around his neck. He seemed in good shape: his hair and beard barely flecked with white; same wide nose as in the old photographs. Photographs like the one taken by Richard Melloul, photographer to the film-stars.

There you see Bokassa, dressed in the uniform of 'Marshal of the Republic', standing in the presidential office and showing to the camera – with a pride he could not conceal – two enormous rough diamonds. He holds them expertly between thumb and forefinger, as if it were perfectly normal for a head of state to keep precious stones in his desk drawer.

Bokassa had not responded to my glance. His eyes remained fixed upon a point in the room which was, as far as I could tell, empty. But at that moment a small girl dressed in a blue school uniform ran in and curled up beside him on the sofa. One of his many daughters, whose names he found it difficult to remember. He addressed her as 'Petite', little one.

Then Jean-Bedel Bokassa turned towards me with a belated show of anger. 'You don't believe me? This crucifix was given to me by the Pope during my visit to the Vatican on 30 July 1970. Shortly before, he baptised me with a special ceremony in his private chapel. He asked if I was prepared to receive a great honour. I said I was and he celebrated the rite. My role in the Catholic Church has been a special, secret one ever since. When I was in power I acted as a mediator for the Vatican in various conflicts, such as that between Libya and Egypt. After my overthrow, the Vatican offered me political asylum. I refused. When I was in prison here in Central Africa, awaiting execution, and then when I was expecting to serve a life sentence, an Italian missionary, Brother Angelino, visited me. We became friends. He gave me a Bible. For seven years it was the only book I read and it made me realise that my being sent to prison was an act of divine grace. Now that the life sentence has been quashed and I'm free, I'm poor, I don't possess anything, not a square metre of land or a single diamond. I don't want anything any more. My only possession is the title of apostle, like Peter and Paul.'

Bokassa fell silent again. Outside, the dazzling heat of the afternoon sun was merciless. The cabinet secretary repeated the date of the Vatican visit, presumably to give the revelation greater credibility: 30 July 1970. The emperor tried to struggle to his feet. His daughter leaped up to help him. In the silence of Villa Nasser, former residence of the Empress Catherine, now reduced to crumbling walls and weed-filled courtyards, he repeated, 'The Pope himself gave me this crucifix. Together with my thirteen Bibles, it is the only thing I have left. Everything else – land, decorations, power, women – belongs to the past. This house, Villa Nasser, I have given to my ex-wife, Madame Catherine, even though she doesn't deserve it after her adultery with Valéry Giscard d'Estaing. The man stole my diamonds and my wife. A pirate. He treated me like that because I am an African. But no matter. Today, thanks to divine intervention, I am a man of peace and faith. Inside, I am still His Majesty Bokassa the First, Apostle of Peace and Servant of Jesus Christ, Emperor and Marshal of Central Africa.'

The following day I accompanied him to the tribunal. He was wearing the same white robe with a narrow buttoned-up collar. The crucifix was around his neck, his hands clasping the cross. Under his arm he carried a framed print of Christ as if it were a lawyer's document-case. Passers-by greeted him respectfully. A few boys in jeans and sunglasses followed us, sniggering among themselves. Bokassa was accompanied by several of his children and the gentleman in tails. Not very far away were the muddy banks of the Obangui River where we could see women washing clothes and fishermen in dugout canoes.

The case before the court was an application for the return of possessions confiscated after the 1979 coup d'état, when French troops – the same troops who had put him in power in 1966 – had forced him into exile. The Bangui government was claiming ownership of his castles in France. The entire Bokassa clan, led by 'Petite', was seated on the public benches. The session was adjourned after a few minutes.

Back at Villa Nasser, he asked me if I would like to take a photograph of him in uniform.

I said yes. But it was unclear if he was referring to the uniform of an Apostle of the Catholic Church or the military variety. He disappeared into one of his rooms, all of which occupied only a corner of the villa.

He emerged into the courtyard wearing a military uniform, the Napoleonic cross of self-appointed marshal on his left breast and seven rows of insignia. He was carrying his ivory-tipped cane, the *canne de justice* that had once descended upon major-domos, ministers, opponents, even his children.

Gazing into space and speaking in a monotone, Bokassa recited his own autobiography.

'My name is Jean-Bedel Bokassa. I was baptised in 1950 at Fréjus, where my old French regiment was based. I received my baptism as thirteenth apostle on 30 July 1970 from Pope Paul VI. I was president from 1966 to 1976. I was, indeed still am, Emperor of Central Africa, being crowned on 4 December 1976. On 20 September 1979 the French removed me from power with a coup d'état. On 20 November 1980 I was condemned to death *in absentia*. In the same year I was extradited to a prison in the Ivory Coast, then extradited to France, where I remained under supervision for two years before being finally repatriated to Central Africa on 23 November 1986. My trial lasted from 23 November 1986 until Friday 2 June 1987, when I was again sentenced to death. The sentence was subsequently commuted, first to life imprisonment and twenty years' forced labour, then to ten years' forced labour. I was finally freed on 1 September 1993. That is the story of my life, that's who I am. I am Jean-Bedel Bokassa. And I no longer have any political ambitions. The present Central African leader is President Patasse.'

The recitation over, Bokassa hurried indoors and changed back into his priestly robe. 'They gave me this robe in prison. It comes from Jerusalem,' he whispered softly. Then repeated, as if in a reverie, 'From Jerusalem. From Jerusalem.'

The real story of his life was naturally rather different.

After the French coup d'état, and following the confiscation of his property by Switzerland and Central Africa, Bokassa lived for several months not in a prison in the Ivory Coast, but in the elegant Villa Cocody at No. 5 Boulevard de la Corniche in Abidjan. The Empress Catherine, having anticipated what was about to happen and having decided to put as much distance as possible between herself and Bokassa, was already safely installed in Geneva. Here she spent much of her time reading Tarot cards. There was talk of her being under the personal protection of Giscard d'Estaing.

The emperor, meanwhile, was in shock. He spent his days playing, at maximum volume, a record called 'Brass Marches and Red *Pompon*' performed by the band of the French navy. Under pressure from France, the president of the Ivory Coast, Felix Houphouët-Boigny, not only gave him the use of the villa, but even arranged with a hotel for meals to be delivered to him twice a day. His old friend Gaddafi had refused to offer him asylum: he had his hands full already with Idi Amin, who had just escaped from Uganda and was now a temporary guest in Tripoli.

From Bangui came news of statues overturned, relatives arrested, houses destroyed, former mistresses fled abroad or absorbed into the harems of the new leaders. One day he received a phone-call from a former French pop singer turned businessman, Bernard Tapie. Bokassa had never met him. A few days later Tapie arrived in Abidjan without an appointment. Having gained entry to the house by bribing the soldiers guarding it, he informed Bokassa that France was about to confiscate all his French properties. These included the Château de Villemorant and that of Saint-Louis Chavanon, the estate known as La Cottencière, Château Handricourt on the outskirts of Paris, a château at Mezy-sur-Seine, a villa in Nice and the hotel-restaurant Le Montague in Romorantin. These properties were the last remnants of Bokassa's possessions. Apart from them he had nothing. Claiming to have the consent of the Élysée and Houphouët-Boigny, Tapie offered to buy the lot for 12.5 million francs. This was less than half their value, but by seven o'clock that evening Bokassa had signed the fatal contract.

Interviewed by the French press a few days later, Tapie admitted that the story of the imminent confiscation was a bluff and declared that he had 'swindled the brutal Bokassa for the good of France'. The emperor sued and, years later, won the case: the contract of sale was declared invalid.

When reciting his own autobiography, Bokassa had omitted to mention a gruesome discovery made at Villa Kolongo. The house, standing on the banks of the river in a district called Kilometre 12 outside Bangui, had been occupied by his Romanian concubine. It was one of Bokassa's favourite residences, with pools, fountains, tropical gardens, an enormous circular rotating bed, ceilings of rare woods and chandeliers of French crystal. French legionaires dispatched from Paris to overthrow him in what was called 'Operation Barracuda' had been ordered to search the house. In the safe they found diamonds and gold watches (set, naturally, with more diamonds). They found several rooms housing the museum that Bokassa had devoted to himself. And in the gigantic freezer adjacent to the kitchens they found dozens of human cadavers, most notably those belonging to the leaders of student organisations. Or so they said.

This was swiftly claimed by the Barracudas as '. . . evidence that he is a cannibal and deserved to be overthrown'.

Bokassa had also omitted to mention that when in power he had granted exclusive rights to trade in ivory to a mysterious Spanish company, La Couronne, in exchange for one-third of the profits – pocketed not by the state but by his family. La Couronne was slaughtering at least 5,000 elephants every year. The diamond trade, at one point assigned to various Saudi and Lebanese associates, brought in more of these lucrative backhanders. As did logging in the forests.

Not for nothing was his preferred self-description that of 'first peasant and first businessman of Central Africa'. In the presidential residences, such as Villa Kolongo and Berengo, Bokassa installed workshops producing textiles and copra. He even had a butchery and a restaurant, both open to the public.

He owned two airlines, two condominiums (Pacifique 1 and Pacifique 2) and a boutique selling clothes made in a factory belonging to his wife Catherine.

Innocent activities, maybe. But he had also forgotten to mention the infamous student massacre.

Impressed by the orderly cadres of Chinese students he had seen during a recent visit to Beijing, and angry at his nation's disappointing results in the 1977 French baccalaureate examinations, Bokassa decided to bring a degree of military discipline to the classrooms of the empire. So on 2 February 1978 the Education Ministry announced that from 1 October all children attending elementary and secondary schools would be required to wear school uniforms designed by Bokassa himself. The girls were to wear dark-blue dresses with light-blue collars and belts, the boys dark-blue trousers and light-blue jackets. Everything was manufactured by the 'Compagnie industrielle oubanguienne des textiles (Ciot)'. Owned by Bokassa. And could be bought only in certain shops. Owned by Bokassa.

The order was ignored. But four months later the Lycée Bokassa and the Lycée Boganda began to turn away children not wearing uniform. On 15 January 1979 3,000 students took to the streets shouting, 'Bokassa, pay our student grants!' and 'After the Shah, Bokassa!' Reza Pahlavi had, in fact, just been driven out of Tehran by the ayatollahs. In Kampala Idi Amin was about to go. The students smashed the windows of Pacifique 2 and took over Bangui.

At six in the evening the imperial guard intervened, led by Bokassa in army fatigues. Over the next twenty-four hours 150 students were mown down by machine-gun fire. Amnesty International protested. Bokassa then broadcast a speech rescinding the order on the wearing of school uniform. A few weeks later Giscard d'Estaing offered the Empire of Central Africa a loan of one billion French African francs – from 'cousin' to 'cousin'.

A few months later it was the university students who took to the streets. Hundreds were arrested. Many were tortured and killed in the notorious Ngaragba prison shortly before Bokassa was overthrown.

In the quasi-epitaph he recited to me, Bokassa had omitted not only the horrific events, but also the ridiculous. Like the solemn announcement to the nation in 1970 that he had awarded himself the title of Grand Master of the International Brotherhood of Knights Collectors of Postage Stamps.

Or the idea of turning up at the Élysée on the day of General de Gaulle's funeral, dressed in the uniform of a parachute regiment, sobbing uncontrollably in front of the general's perplexed widow and moaning, *'Mon père, mon papa*. I lost my natural father when I was a child. Now I have lost my adoptive father as well. I am an orphan again.'

He was quite unaware that de Gaulle ridiculed him, calling him *le soudard* ('squaddie') or 'Papa Bock' – the Papa Doc of Africa, a beer-swilling Duvalier.

'God has absolved me. The people of Central Africa have absolved me, too. Now I don't owe anything to anybody. Neither to God nor to the people. We're quits. My people saved me. If the accusations spread by the French about me had been true, I would not be alive today. In Africa one pays with one's life for evil deeds like cannibalism. I obeyed my people. I disobeyed France. And for that they stripped me of power.'

I interrupted Bokassa, reminding him about May 1968. When, on a tide of student unrest, de Gaulle left Paris for a safer location, *'le soudard'* rushed to Radio-Bangui and launched an absurd appeal from the heart of colonial Africa: 'The hero of 1940, the hero of 1958, the liberator of France, the liberator of Africa should not be intimidated but should remain in power.'

'Yes, I stayed loyal to France,' the emperor acknowledged. 'But did I have a choice? My grandfather pushed me into enlisting when I was eighteen because in every royal family such as mine the heir had to know how to fight.'

The former emperor had a talent for embellishing the past. His father, for example, was a village chief rather than a king.

46

Bokassa did not see the distinction and kept on about the French. 'They wanted it all their own way, they wanted to sell us their products at hugely inflated prices and buy our raw materials for a pittance. For years the French vetoed the construction of a cement plant in Central Africa in order to export their own cement. The English were different: they colonised in a more honest way. The only Africans in power today are the puppets of France. But you can't build a nation like that. I built up this nation in thirteen years. And that did not please France.'

The interview was resumed the following day at Villa Nasser, again in the presence of an array of medicines. This time I was accompanied by Raphael Kopessoua, the Central African Radio journalist who had introduced me to the former emperor. I had found his name on dispatches sent from Bangui by the Associated Press. Kopessoua was their local stringer. On the phone he had sounded less than enthusiastic, but had finally agreed and said, 'Come to Bangui and I will do what I can to help you.'

Raphael was the silent type and poker-faced. Despite the humid heat he invariably wore a jacket and tie and always carried a leather briefcase stuffed full of papers. I collected him every morning from the radio station, a green building with no doors and no windows. The mouldering plaster was falling off in chunks. There were no chairs in the offices. I saw neither microphones nor any other broadcasting equipment, only heavy typewriters.

Restless and suspicious, Raphael gave the impression of being in a state of constant alarm. Although head of the syndicate of Central African journalists, there was no love lost between him and his radio colleagues, many of whom were related to politicians and rarely turned up to work. He brightened up, indeed seemed almost happy, only when describing for my benefit the power struggles in Bangui. Grubby deals and extortion rackets, greedy army officers and corrupt ministers. Banished one day and in government the next. A breathtaking *danse macabre*.

47

Years afterwards I was to read about Raphael in the English and American press. He had become the director of a weekly opposition magazine and had been thrown into prison for two months for having 'defamed the head of state', Ange Felix Patasse, once Bokassa's prime minister, later his opponent and finally his successor.

Towards Bokassa, on the other hand, Raphael seemed strangely well disposed. He even nodded in agreement when the former emperor boasted, in yet another rant about ranks, titles, hierarchies, 'Of all the African leaders I was the greatest. Why? Because I was the emperor. One step below me was the king of Morocco. A king and a great head of state. Then came all the others: simple presidents.'

'I was the emperor . . .' Bokassa repeated, again gazing into space.

It was still an obsession, after all these years. In 1978, at the annual summit of Francophone African nations, Bokassa had asked that French protocol ensure that he was addressed as 'Your Imperial Majesty' and put first in order of precedence. The French diplomats had refused the request. Only the president of Gabon, Omar Bongo, was in favour, because he too had imperial ambitions.

I tried to press Bokassa on the subject of Giscard's famous diamonds. Why had Bokassa given them to him? The emperor looked at me as if I was mad. 'He asked for them. Besides, I was his friend, almost like a relative. He came to Central Africa twice a year. I supplied him with virgin women and virgin territory, where he shot dozens of elephants without paying a single franc. Sometimes he came with his mistresses, some famous, some not. And I gave him diamonds. He wanted lots. To give to his mistresses. There you have your answer.'

I returned to the apostle business. He came out with a new revelation. 'At twelve years old – yes, at twelve years old, at twelve – I had three visions of Christ. When I went to Rome I informed the Pope. And he, forty years after the visions, baptised me as an apostle.'

I decided to pass on to other matters. Was it true that he was strengthening relations with the Soviet Union before the French coup?

'I've been to the Soviet Union several times. Several times. I've made several visits to the Soviet Union. They made me an honorary member of the Soviet navy in Sevastopol on the Black Sea.' He concluded by informing me that 'Sevastopol is a city on the Black Sea'.

Baptised by the Pope. Baptised by the Russians. I was beginning to feel sorry for the former emperor. Kopessoua remained inscrutable. I asked Bokassa about the medals and the jewels, two subjects close to his heart. The emperor replied simply, 'All stolen by the French. Now all I have is this cross.' Then he began to list the names of the French officers who had taken part in Operation Barracuda, accusing them of having appropriated his imperial képi, his pearls, his clothes. When he got to the end of the list, he repeated, 'I am prepared to go and live in poverty with my children in the market at Kilometre 5, on the street. This house is Catherine's. Beautiful woman, but with a cold heart.'

He sighed like a boy in love. 'I've had the most beautiful women in the world. So I forgive Catherine, because her beauty was a ray of sunshine in my life. If she comes back I will hand over Villa Nasser to her and go and live on the streets. At Kilometre 5.'

The following day we ourselves were out on the red earth roads of Central Africa. We had hired a car to tour the imperial residences. A friend of Raphael's, or a relative perhaps, was at the wheel.

Leaving Bangui, one has to pass what was once the Bokassa Stadium, an oval of cracked concrete. The stadium was deserted. No one in Bangui appeared to play football any more. This was the same Palais des Sports where the emperor's coronation had taken place. (The Vatican had refused permission to use the cathedral.) This was where the presidential guard had held its march-pasts. And where, in 1986, the second trial had started. A trial during which Bokassa was accused of cannibalism, misappropriation of public funds, concealment of children's bodies and ten further charges.

People avoided that sinister Colosseum.

The road leading out of Bangui first wound around the Palais. At the last moment I asked Raphael to pull over. Under an arch of crumbling concrete was Bokassa's famous throne. Rusty but perfectly recognisable. Still in the shape of a Napoleonic eagle, three and a half metres high with two huge golden wings. Papa Bock had had it constructed in France and placed in the middle of the stadium for the coronation ceremony. The throne itself, on which he was sitting surrounded by ermine pelts and swathes of red velvet when he seized the crown and put it on his own head, was carved out of the belly of the eagle.

The throne was still there. Forgotten. Wingless. Reduced to a skeleton. But still standing. Like its master.

Just beyond a roadblock two kilometres outside Bangui, we ran over a large porcupine. Raphael got out and dumped it into the boot of the car. 'Delicious roasted,' he said.

The motorway between Bangui and Berengo was the first and last motorway built in the country. Eighty kilometres long, it was now reduced to a single lane that was all potholes. The only other traffic we encountered consisted of two cars and three lorries. After driving for two hours we reached Bokassa's African Versailles. It seemed impossible that only a few years earlier those crumbling walls had enclosed an imperial court with a rigid protocol copied from that of the Shah of Persia.

Bokassa had built a self-sufficient compound with farms, herds of cattle, staff quarters, offices, private houses and flats for foreign visitors furnished with reproduction antique furniture and gilt mirrors. Here he convened the Imperial Council, a second government that counted for far more than the official one led by Patasse.

It had all been looted many years previously. Berengo had

become a ghost town. The floors were strewn with Kalashnikov bullets. Vegetation had invaded the empty rooms where, in 1977, the British journalist Michael Goldsmith had been beaten personally by Bokassa until the blood ran and then forced to sign a 'confession' stating that he was a South African spy. The fields were empty. But the decrepit walls still bore the painted letters JBB, laurel wreaths in the style of Caesar Augustus and the motto of the empire, '*Dignité, Unité, Travail*'. I wondered in which of these rooms the heir to the throne, his favourite son, Prince Saint-Jean de Bokassa de Berengo de Boubangui de Centrafrique, had played.

Raphael suggested that we visit one of the bungalows near the entrance to the estate. It was where the custodian lived. He asked where I came from and invited us to dinner, which consisted of one of the chickens that roamed around the ex-imperial courtyards. His wife served us silently, not sitting down to the table herself. Then, at the end of the meal, her duty done, she spoke at last, in perfect Italian. She had just returned from Rome, where she had worked as a housemaid for many years. A city, she remarked – without a hint of irony – that reminded her of Berengo because it had once been the seat of another imperial court and also had some interesting archaeological ruins.

On our return journey we hit a small antelope, which ran out suddenly from the bushes. Far from swerving round it, Kopessoua's friend deliberately ran over it. Raphael got out and put it in the boot of the car with the other prey. 'Delicious roasted,' he remarked.

Our last stop was at Bangui's only real tourist attraction, Villa Kilongo, at Kilometre 12. A group of baby-faced soldiers took us to see the villa where the Romanian woman, the most prominent of Bokassa's concubines, and the babysitter Martine N'Douta had been found in bed with soldiers of the garrison. Martine was killed immediately. The Romanian was warned, but defended herself by accusing Bokassa of ignoring her in favour of the Vietnamese and Gabonese concubines, his current favourites. Bokassa had first threatened to throw the men to the crocodiles, then relented to the point of having them humanely killed in prison.

Kilongo, with its courtyards and fountains, was like a Mexican hacienda. The ceiling of the banqueting hall had been dismantled. There was no longer any sign of the long table at which, according to statements made by David Dacko, twice president and a cousin of Bokassa, fillet of opposition leader was once served.

The soldiers marched us round the perimeter of the estate where Bokassa and the Romanian dancer, seated on a kind of altar, improvised summary trials of their enemies, real or presumed. Emperor and ballerina decided the method of execution, deliberating between the firing squad (in constant readiness), the prison with its inevitable diseases and the crocodiles.

Apart from cadavers in the kitchens, the legionaires said they found human bones at the bottom of Villa Kilongo's swimming pools.

The swimming pools were still discernible, their blue tiles now buried beneath layers of soil. At one point the youngest of the soldiers scrambled down into the smallest of the pools. After scrabbling about under the weeds, he pulled out a smooth white bone, declaring, 'Human. Eaten by Bokassa. One hundred francs.' Raphael seized the bone and studied it for a couple of seconds before pronouncing, 'Goat. Delicious roasted.' Faced with such unshakeable certainty, the soldier gave up arguing and conceded, 'Okay. Goat. But eaten by Bokassa.'

On 29 July 1972 the following order, Decree No. 29.058, was issued by the Republic of Central Africa:

Any person discovered in the act of theft shall be subject to the following punishments:
1. The first time such an offence is committed one ear shall be amputated.
2. The second time such an offence is committed the other ear shall be amputated.

3. The third time such an offence is committed one hand shall be amputated.
Amputations will be performed by suitably qualified surgeons within 24 hours of sentence being passed.

On several occasions the decree was put into practice, in the middle of the market square at Kilometre 5. In full public view. Bokassa – who was at the time president-for-life, minister of defence, justice, home affairs, agriculture, health and aviation – presided over the amputations. The secretary-general of the United Nations, Kurt Waldheim, protested. Bokassa's reply described him as 'a ruffian, a colonialist', and, strangely, as 'an imperialist'.

New Year's Eve 1985 was the twentieth anniversary of the coup that carried Bokassa to power. He spent it in the Château Handricourt in France, west of Paris. The vast rooms with their portraits of the Empress Catherine, busts of Napoleon and photographs of the battle of Dien Bien Phu (with the legend: 'They gave their lives for Liberty') were cold. There was no money for heating. 'I haven't got the money to feed the fifteen children who live here with me,' he told journalists. 'Every day more bills arrive and I don't know how to pay them.'

Bokassa was, in fact, a penniless prisoner, prevented from selling his châteaux because the Central African Republic had laid legal claim to them, and forbidden to leave Handricourt by the French secret services. A book that he wrote, *Ma Verité*, was pulped on the orders of Giscard d'Estaing before it reached the shops.

Six months later, however, the situation seemed to change completely. The tribunal in Paris gave him back the Corvette, a plane worth six million francs that had been sequestrated by the Central African Republic after Operation Barracuda. And the gendarmes guarding the entrance to the château were recalled. Now the former emperor found new French friends, a lawyer and two former officers close to the extreme right. Thanks to them, the Corvette was sold and the proceeds invested in another plan: escape.

On 21 October 1986 Bokassa told his wife Augustine (whom he had met in the Ivory Coast) that they would be returning to Bangui next day, on a scheduled Air Afrique flight, using forged papers. During the flight someone informed the captain about his famous passenger. But the captain, assuming that if Bokassa were indeed on board it must be with the permission of the French government, saw no reason to disrupt the journey.

On arrival at Bangui, no one recognised him at first. Then, in the baggage hall, someone shouted, 'It's Bokassa!' The crowd began to buzz. 'The boss is back . . . Get to the presidential palace! Get to the presidential palace!' The terrified police took to their heels. The crowd applauded. Bokassa began to make a speech.

Twenty minutes later Colonel Jean-Claude Mantion, on secondment from Paris to command the new presidential guard, arrived in the baggage hall, followed by dozens of soldiers. He arrested Bokassa, suspecting that the former emperor's return to Bangui signalled his intention to seize power once again.

'I'm here just to clear my name,' he protested. Eight months later Bokassa was sentenced to execution. No one, however, could explain why he had left Handricourt.

'It was the French secret service. They kidnapped me, my then concubine and my children and put us on the first plane to Bangui,' Bokassa told me. He actually used the word 'concubine'. And he continued, 'I still have the names of all the officers in charge of the operation.' He had forgotten about the letter he wrote to President François Mitterand on the eve of his departure, which began: 'I return a free man to a free nation. And if I am invited to be of service to it, I shall accept immediately, because my dearest wish is to serve the people. Indeed, to serve all men: a philosophical concept natural to those of us imbued with French culture.'

★   ★   ★

The crippled children encamped in front of Bangui's one and only hotel had learned to recognise me. Every time they saw me they greeted me with cries of '*Bonjour!*'

The hotel, belonging to a French chain, stood on the banks of the river. French soldiers in fatigues sat in the bar every evening. They spoke about Rwanda, but only among themselves. Every now and then a girl dressed in yellow came to visit them. She would come barefoot as far as the hotel door, clutching her very high-heeled shoes – also yellow – under her arm. The leader of the crippled children always watched the little ceremony. He addressed her as 'sister', earning a tip from the soldiers.

At his home close to the cathedral Bokassa often referred to 'the fruit of my blood'. I assumed he was referring to the child he called Petite and of whom he seemed especially fond. Until I realised that he was referring to his pension, that of a French army captain, earned partly by 'six months in a military hospital in Indo-China'. The pension enabled him to survive. It also enabled more than a hundred of his legitimate and illegitimate children, spread over Africa and France, to survive.

The heir to the throne, 'prince' Jean-Bedel Georges Bokassa, lives in Versailles – no other place would suit him, of course – and was recently sentenced to one year of prison for a financial fraud of about £30,000.

There was the Romanian, the Tunisian, the Gabonese, the French, the Vietnamese, the Belgian, the Libyan, the Cameroonian, the German, the Swede, the Zairese, the Chinese ('a present' from Chiang Kai-shek). And obviously Catherine, the empress.

Bokassa's women were the only visible result of his frequent official visits abroad. They were often 'given' to him by foreign heads of state as a token of friendship. Sometimes he saw them when out and about, and asked for them to be introduced to him. If he liked them he took them back to Bangui. Each would be installed in a separate villa. Each would be obliged to await the attentions of the master.

He met the Gabonese at the airport in Libreville at the end of an official tour. She was among the throng of notables who had come to see him off. She was very beautiful. According to the magazine *Jeune Afrique*, Bokassa whispered to her not to move from where she was. 'I'll be right back.' Then he embraced President Omar Bongo and boarded his plane.

Fifteen minutes later he commanded the captain of the presidential jet to do an about-turn. Bongo, who was already being driven away from the airport, was informed that Bokassa had changed his mind. He returned precipitately to the airport, where a smiling Bokassa reassured him, 'Earlier I was here as a head of state. Now I'm here in a private capacity. And I'm about to marry one of your fellow citizens.' A few hours later the Gabonese, Joelle, was in Bangui.

Most famous of all his concubines was the Romanian. Bokassa's eye had lighted upon the blonde dancer in a Bucharest nightclub during a visit to his ally Nicolae Ceausescu. Her name was Gabriela Drimba. At first she refused to marry Bokassa. But some weeks later she turned up in Bangui. And immediately became the stuff of legend.

Most mysterious were the three Vietnamese women. One was Bokassa's wife. Two were his daughters. One daughter was real, the other false. Both bore the name Martine Nguyen. They came to Bangui from Vietnam after Bokassa had searched (with the help of the French government) for his daughter by the wife he married in Saigon in 1953 and then abandoned. The first to arrive in Bangui was the False Martine. But she was exposed as a fraud. The French press fell on the story, ridiculing the 'ogre of Central Africa'. Bokassa responded to his critics by adopting the girl, to show the world how generous he was. Then he found the Real Martine working in a Vietnamese cement factory. She too was persuaded to leave Vietnam for Africa.

Once in Bangui, Bokassa offered both of them in marriage via a kind of public auction. Hundreds of young Central African men bid for them. The eventual winners of the competition were a doctor and an army officer. The sumptuous wedding in the cathedral was even attended by a few heads of state, the most prominent being the ever-faithful Omar Bongo.

The False Martine's husband, the army officer, eventually attempted a coup and was shot. The Real Martine's husband, the doctor, remained loyal to Bokassa. He too was shot, but by Bokassa's enemies after Operation Barracuda.

One day, tired of talking about his military experiences, the emperor returned to the subject of the Bible. He recited the Lord's Prayer. He compared Christ to Nelson Mandela, saying, 'He suffered a lot in prison, like me. Mandela is a gift of God to the African people, to compensate them for centuries of suffering.' And he revealed that he had seen the Italian prime minister Silvio Berlusconi on television just after he was elected. 'I liked him immediately.'

On my last visit to Villa Nasser I found Bokassa alone, holding a Bible. I still had to ask him about the most serious charge, the one that worried him most. 'The story about cannibalism was invented in order to destroy me. It's a lie. Do you really believe that a much-decorated French officer could be a cannibal? It's a lie,' he repeated. And indeed the famous trial cleared him on this charge. But what about the other crimes? The murders. Bokassa did not deny them. 'But I was not the only one. What about Ariel Sharon? Why has he been forgiven for the massacres at Shabra and Shatila, while I have been forgiven for nothing? Just because I'm African?'

He seemed in good form that day. Perhaps he had taken his medicines.

Jean-Bedel Bokassa died on 3 November 1996, two years after our meeting. He is buried at Berengo. In its obituary, Central African state radio described him as 'illustrious'. Ten years ago, during his disgrace, the same radio called him 'the Ogre of Berengo'.

The Empress Catherine lives in Lausanne and refuses to speak about Bokassa.

Giscard d'Estaing remains an influential politician. Few still remember the scandal over the diamonds.

Bernard Tapie has been successively a minister, a convict and the owner of the Olympique Marseilles football team, which he had to sell, but to which he has subsequently returned. He now works as an actor, his real vocation all along, as Bokassa learned the hard way.

Patasse is president of the Republic of Central Africa. He has allied himself with Gaddafi.

The Romanian dancer has returned to Bucharest, leaving her daughter, Anne de Berengo, behind in Bangui. Nothing more has been heard of her.

The Real Martine managed to escape from Bangui after the coup. She now runs a Vietnamese restaurant in Paris.

The False Martine was killed by Bokassa's bodyguards a year after her husband's failed coup.

Augustine, the last 'concubine', has returned to Handricourt, where she now lives with several of the former emperor's children. She still struggles to pay the bills.

Omar Bongo has been president of Gabon since 1969. A wealthy man (unlike surviving members of Bokassa's family), he has been one of the main private clients of Citibank since 1970.

Ariel Sharon is prime minister of Israel.

Raphael Kopessoua is not, for the moment, in prison.

Jaruzelski

No snowflake in the avalanche ever feels responsible.

Stanislaw Jerzy Lec

When he came to power, his identikit was almost a stereotype of the military leader of a banana republic. He appeared on television claiming 'to stand for law and order' and promising an end to the 'chaos' into which the country had fallen 'due to a handful of extremists'. Subsequently he spoke little and then reluctantly, his inscrutable expression giving nothing away except for the fact that here was a man of action who disliked wasting time in discussion and would not tolerate dissent. His thin lips were habitually pursed into a supercilious, angry expression. Above all, there were his two trademarks, the standard olive-green uniform of a general, impeccably pressed with rows of ribbons on the chest, and the large dark glasses, almost completely hiding his severe, schoolmasterly face.

This was in February 1981, and for the international press the story was a carbon-copy of many others. In Chile, for example, another minister of defence in famously sinister dark glasses had installed himself as prime minister after a rapid rise to power and with not dissimilar ambitions. In 1973 General Augusto Pinochet's aim was to 'restore order and the Chilean identity' in sunny Santiago. In 1981 General Wojciech Jaruzelski was determined to 'restore social order and defend Socialism' in the snowy streets of Warsaw. They were both soldiers whom 'exceptional circumstances' had forced to enter politics and put themselves 'at the service of the country'. Both proclaimed that 'the armed forces are beloved by our fellow citizens over all other institutions'. Both were at the beck and call of a Big Brother, Chile being on the threshold of a tragic dictatorship backed by the United States, Poland on the threshold of a tragic dictatorship backed by a bloc of the Soviet Union's vassal states called – ironically – the 'Warsaw Pact'.

Even contemporary photographs show a disquieting similarity between the two generals, but the Poland of General Wojciech Jaruzelski was very different from the Chile of General Augusto Pinochet. The biggest difference lay in the fact that the ancient Catholic land of Poland had just given the Church of Rome its new Pope. The first non-Italian Pope, in fact, for four and a half centuries.

Three years earlier, on 16 October 1978, Karol Wojtyla, the young cardinal-archbishop of Cracow, had been unexpectedly elected to the papal throne. The plume of white smoke issuing from the Sistine Chapel had sent shivers of apprehension throughout the Socialist countries barricaded behind the 'Iron Curtain'. Jaruzelski's Poland, one of the bastions of the Soviet bloc, was now also – or maybe overridingly – the Pope's Poland. Wojtyla's Poland.

As Soviet bastions go, Poland was not the gloomiest by a long chalk. One well-known witticism even referred to it as 'the jolliest of all the barracks in the Communist concentration camp'. One where, in the absence of consumer goods, the inmates kept their spirits up with laughter.

Jaruzelski had immediately become one of the easiest victims of this sense of humour. One quip ran, 'Do you know why Jaruzelski always wears protective glasses?' – 'No.' – 'Because he's trying to weld Poland to the Soviet Union.'

There was more than a grain of truth in this. Jaruzelski dreamed not only of a firm military bond, but also of historical and sentimental bonds with Mother Russia and the Slav countries to the east of his own borders, seeing this as the only alternative to subjugation by the Germanic powers to the west.

Caught historically and geographically between the two

giants, Germany and Russia, Jaruzelski's Poland was the child of the Molotov-Ribbentrop Pact by which Nazi Germany and the Soviet Union divided eastern Europe between them just days before the outbreak of the Second World War. Nominally a non-aggression pact, this did not stop Adolf Hitler advancing upon Leningrad, invading Poland en route and driving a wedge between its two souls, the West-orientated and the East-orientated. One Polish volunteer force, led by the staunch anti-Communist General Wladyslaw Anders, assisted American and British troops in the liberation of Italy. Another volunteer force, led by the pro-Russian General Zygmund Berling, allied itself with the Soviet forces and took part in the liberation of Poland itself and of Berlin.

Like many other young upper-class men, Wojciech Jaruzelski had inadvertently found himself in the force commanded by Berling.

Now seventy-eight, Jaruzelski no longer wears uniform, but has retained the second of his trademarks, the dark glasses. The general, who walks with the aid of a black stick yet holds himself as upright as any soldier, is a tormented man. He speaks in the measured tones of a university lecturer, dresses in an unremarkable fawn suit of East European cut and a rather loud tie, but every now and then an angry gesture hints at many more angry gestures diligently repressed. Confronted with a statement he considers inaccurate, or a question posited upon such a statement, he raises the famous, almost diabolically long eyelashes and waves his hands in the air. 'Read this,' he says coldly. And tosses a letter on to the table, or a legal deposition, or some other document relating to his time in power that supports his argument. Or he points to two slim volumes – one in green, the other in orange covers – published at his own expense and written in the form of a legal argument addressed to an imaginary tribunal of History.

The Poles, even those who support him, see him as a tragic figure. A victim of circumstances which presented him, as leader, with impossible choices, all of which were wrong. An old man who ended up morally and politically defeated despite all his efforts to convince his fellow countrymen that he deserved their respect.

A joke going the rounds during the final years of Socialist rule said that the general, still in power but already an unhappy, embittered man, was complaining to his driver about the inexplicable – inexplicable to him – unpopularity he suffered. 'It would take a miracle to make the Polish people love me,' he said. The driver, who in secret was obviously a devout Catholic and a member of Solidarity, relayed the conversation to his guardian angel. And the angel had a word with the general. 'Leave it to me, Mr President. I'll give you the power to perform a miracle. You will walk on water.' So early one morning the general and his driver went to the banks of the Vistula, the river that runs through the capital. Jaruzelski tried to put one foot in the water. To his surprise, the foot stayed on the surface. He tried with the other foot. Same result. So he set off, walking on the water. Two fishermen, typically irreverent Varsarvians, spotted him as they stood nearby enjoying a glass of beer. 'Hey look! That's Jaruzelski,' says one of them. 'So it is,' says the other. 'And how pathetic! Can't even swim.'

Not even a miracle could persuade the Polish people to forgive the general for two misdeeds, which he himself blames on a culprit under investigation for thousands of years, but difficult to put behind bars: History.

The first unforgivable action occurred in December 1970, when he was minister of defence. His troops fired on workers taking part in the first anti-government demonstrations in the shipyards at Gdansk and Gdynia. Forty-four demonstrators were killed, thousands wounded. The trial arising from this episode began in 1996 and is expected to continue for some time yet. Jaruzelski maintains that he never gave the order to fire. That, he says, came from the prime minister of the time, Wladyslaw Gomulka, who had dismissed him from his post as army chief.

The second occurred in 1981, also in the fateful month of

December. Only a few months into his premiership, Jaruzelski declared martial law, announcing on television that he had assumed power on behalf of the Military Council for National Salvation, a body that no one had ever heard of before that moment. Immediately a whole raft of restrictions came into force. Solidarnosc, or Solidarity – the trade-union movement sprung in 1980 from the 1970 workers' movement – was banned for fear that its membership of ten million and its enormous popularity would encourage it to bid for power. Its charismatic leader, the electrician Lech Walesa, was silenced.

The army was in control of the whole country. Strikes were outlawed, with ten years' imprisonment for those who flouted the order. All telephone communication was temporarily disabled. A 10 p.m. curfew was imposed. Tanks appeared on the streets of Warsaw and every major city. Writers, intellectuals, journalists, theatre producers, trade unionists and dissident priests were arrested. Relations with the Church became tense. Television newsreaders were obliged to wear army uniform when reading the news. Programmes were reduced to a litany of patriotic songs, military parades and classical music. During the long period of repression that followed, hundreds of dissidents were incarcerated.

The Kremlin breathed a sigh of relief. Leonid Brezhnev was convinced that the cancer of rebellion had been excised and that the danger of its spreading to other member countries in the Warsaw Pact was over.

Twenty years later the military takeover is still considered a watershed in the country's long history. Jaruzelski might have saved the regime, but he lost the hearts of the people.

When Solidarity came to power, public opinion put pressure on its leaders – who were reluctant to reopen old wounds – until they filed a case against Jaruzelski and other former politicians. The hearings ended in 1996 with the government acquitting Jaruzelski.

Public opinion absolved him too, but it has not forgiven him. The general knows this and his sense of its unfairness makes him profoundly despondent. He was, he argues, forced to introduce martial law in order to forestall military intervention by the Soviet army. 'If I had not acted and opted for the lesser of two evils, on 13 December 1981 Warsaw could have become another Budapest 1956, with more Soviet tanks on the streets of a European capital.'

Today Jaruzelski occupies a small office – two rooms – located on the most Soviet-style avenue in Warsaw, the Jerozolimskie. From the window you can see the Palace of Culture, a horrible, lugubrious skyscraper presented by Joseph Stalin to the Polish people in 1952 as a tangible – and unmistakable – sign of Soviet domination. Now the Soviet Union is gone. But Stalin's 'present' is still the highest building in Warsaw. Constructed using forty million bricks, it can be seen from a distance of twenty kilometres. Like Jaruzelski it has, since the beginning, been hated and loved in equal proportions by a country whose attitude to Russia has always been ambivalent, a mixture of admiration and fear, brotherhood and rivalry.

The office is his by right, as a former head of state, and is funded by the government. The same applies to his secretary, who speaks perfect Russian and spends most of her time maintaining Jaruzelski's links with the former leaders of the Soviet bloc with whom he has remained on friendly terms. The government also pays for his two bodyguards. Jaruzelski receives a monthly salary of five thousand zloty. Not a large sum. But the state also provides him with a car and a dacha in the Masurian lake district, in the grounds of a military base once used as a summer holiday resort or weekend retreat for the Polish *Nomenklatura*. Anxious to imitate their Soviet opposite numbers, in this as in other respects.

The general has a modest lifestyle. He goes to the theatre every so often with his wife, a university lecturer in philology who has never taken any interest in politics and has hardly ever appeared in public. They have a daughter. They still attend receptions at the Russian Embassy. And the general spends hour after hour poring over the papers relating to his trial and polishing letters of complaint to the press – rarely published – contradicting historical accounts that he deems inaccurate.

'The newspapers have already pronounced their verdict, but I remind those armchair historians sitting comfortably at home in their slippers that it was not I who decreed the historical circumstances. I only had the unenviable task of choosing the lesser of two evils. Whatever my decision, the results would have been negative. Mine were difficult decisions. No one has the right to dismiss me lightly as a murderer. I am a patriot. I saved Poland from grave danger. In December 1981 the Soviets were about to trample all over us. Even Gorbachev said so many times over.' He rises from his yellow leatherette office chair to look for a letter, a hand-written document with much underlining in red. Then he cracks one of his rare jokes. He follows it with a wry comment: 'My sense of humour is rapidly deteriorating. A combination of advancing age and interminable legal battles.'

Snow is falling outside. The temperature has dropped to $-15°C$. The only softening touch in the room is a small print of a horse's head. The general, unexpectedly aristocratic for a Communist leader, has been passionately fond of horses ever since he was serving as a young officer on the eastern front. This is the only distraction of a disciplinarian proud of his ability to work a fifteen-hour day in the office. The secretary enters the room and interrupts our conversation. 'Mr President, Gorbachev would like a word.'

The two former leaders, both bitter about the lack of appreciation shown by their respective peoples, both destined to go down in history as the last ranking representatives of old-style Socialism, exchange New Year greetings. All around them Christmas is being celebrated by two deeply religious nations, but the general and the Politburo reformist, still aloof and out of touch after all these years, remain staunchly atheist and make a point of concerning themselves only with the secular festivity.

★   ★   ★

'I am innocent of all wrongdoing. To explain why I am convinced of this, I must begin with the story of my life and the big paradox with which it began. My feelings for Russia and the Soviet Union should have been those of hatred, but they developed in a completely different way. I was raised in a family where anti-Russian views were strongly held, as was traditionally the case in my social class, which was that of the landed gentry. My grandfather took part in the famous anti-Tsarist insurrection of January 1863. He was sentenced to twelve years in Siberia. I carry his surname. My father fought in the 1920 war between Russia and Poland. I was meant to be like them. To carry on the tradition. So I was sent to the school run by the Marian Fathers in Warsaw, where every subject – history, geography, languages – was linked to the tragic history of relations between Poland and Russia. Indeed, if I may digress for a moment, somebody once said that the Marian Order now has two generals: the Superior General, who is the very reverend Adam Boniecki, a close collaborator of Pope John Paul II, and the General, full stop. Jaruzelski.

'But to return to my own story. Everything I was taught, about literature, theatre, books and art, instilled a very negative attitude towards Russia and the Soviet bloc. Then on top of this came the deportations to Siberia. My father was arrested and sent to a *lager*, a Siberian labour camp. He survived, but when he returned he was a broken man and he died in 1946. I was sent to Siberia too, together with my mother and my sister. I was seventeen, my sister twelve. What were we accused of? Nothing. We had committed no crime at all. Apart from belonging to a certain milieu, that of the upper class. Those punishing us were the Soviet authorities, who were by then in charge of a large part of Poland. Following the Molotov-Ribbentrop pact, at least fifteen million Poles found themselves living in what had become *de facto* a region of the Soviet Union. In Siberia I began to work very hard. I felled trees. The cold was indescribable.

'All this constituted the "critical mass" which should have made me hate the Russians.

'Paradoxically, the very opposite began to happen. I fell in love with the Russians, with their indomitable spirit, with the country itself and its culture. I got to know the simple people, the ordinary people of the taiga. They worked and suffered like I did. I realised that they were not the monsters my education had led me to expect. Nor were they the monsters of traditional Polish literature or the stories told around the family fireside. Many of them were very forthcoming, people who liked to meet you man-to-man, were very honest with everyone. Many years later I had the chance to compare the treatment of the Poles deported to Germany with that of the prisoners sent to forced-labour camps in Russia. The former were treated like second-class citizens. In Russia, in Siberia, all were equal.

'I was also able to see how they behaved and how willing they were to make sacrifices, to put up with the situation they found themselves in, that long and terrible war. I saw how they were able to work despite the cold, in temperatures of minus twenty degrees, protected only by canvas tents, assembling aircraft, tanks, canons. Thinking only of the battlefront, of the soldiers who needed those armaments to defend the Motherland. Even small boys, old men, women too. After cutting down the trees, I supplied some of the hospitals with firewood, and there I met people who had been disabled in the war and wounded soldiers brought back from the front. I began to appreciate their patriotism. Their eagerness to fight for their country. Their readiness for self-sacrifice.

'During that period I also began to warm to them through my discovery of great Russian literature. Yes, people were reading books even in the most isolated wastes of Siberia and there were libraries where you could find the works of Chekhov, Tolstoy, Turgenev . . . I still didn't know much Russian, but I learned the language from those books. I read at night by a very feeble, low-powered light, sometimes only a candle. A practice that, combined with the blinding reflections off the Siberian snow, ruined my eyesight and forced me to wear, as an adult, these dark glasses with which I am always identified. Some people assumed that I didn't want to be looked in the eye. But it was a medical condition, not shyness or arrogance.

'My mother tried to dissuade me. She would say, "That's enough, it's time you were asleep." But although I only understood one word in four, I wouldn't give in. I made myself go on reading into the small hours. I hid under the blankets. I hadn't realised it, but I was already becoming like your average Russian, who reads voraciously, continuously. Many years later I woke up to the fact that when Russians travel, be it by bus, train or underground, they always carry a book with them.

'In the books I discovered the other Russian soul. Besides the spirit of the Russians who worked with me in the woods, felling trees, living the hard life of the forest, there was the Russian soul of the ruling class that Tolstoy described. I identified with both. But the point of no return came when I found myself in the army. My superiors, my colleagues and those who depended on me were all Russian. I fought alongside them. I saw their courage and their comradeship. We advanced together as far as Berlin, which we liberated in May 1945.

'Some people have criticised me for having fought with General Berling instead of General Anders. But the explanation of my choice is simple: there was no choice. As in the case of the dark glasses. As in the case of many other things that have happened in my life: I really had no choice.

'On this issue, for instance, as soon as I heard that Anders was recruiting a fighting force, I tried to enrol. I went to a Polish consulate, where I was told to wait: they were giving precedence to those with previous military experience. I obeyed. When I tried again a few months later, Anders had already left and the only thing I could do was enrol with Berling. That's another paradox in my life. The sons of peasants, working men and humble policemen who had stayed in Poland ended up with Anders, who was pro-Western, while men like me, from the professional classes and the aristocracy, sons of high-ranking officers and well-to-do families, because they had been deported to the Soviet Union and could not reach

Anders, found themselves with the pro-Soviet Berling. We were fighting against the interests of our own past. We sided with those who had confiscated the lands and palaces of our own families.

'So when I marched into Berlin I possessed nothing. Everything I owned was in my pockets.

'My men and I marched through Poland liberating it as we went, and were among the first to enter Berlin, side-by-side with the Russians. That was one of the proudest moments of my career. These are all things that forge really strong links. Obviously I cannot help remembering the wrong that was done to my family. However, I have reached the conclusion that it was the price we had to pay for the enormous upheaval taking place during the period when I was growing to manhood.

'Choosing to make a career in the army, I have had many contacts with the Russians. I also had the opportunity to get to know Russia as a world power. I visited the Baikonur space centre, in Kazakhstan. I became better acquainted with their culture. So, if we want a concrete illustration – if someone asks me where I got to know the Russians and learned to love them – I reply that it happened in four places: in the Siberian taiga, the front-line trenches, the Baikonur space centre and the Bolshoi.'

Jaruzelski's office is close to Warsaw station, in a street famous for brothels where the prostitutes are from the Ukraine, Russia, Belorussia, Romania, Bulgaria and Moldavia. A new Eastern bloc, a new Warsaw Pact that papers the city with its own propaganda in the shape of glossy leaflets showing nude women offering Christmas bargains and specifying '*trzecia godzina gratis*' – 'third hour free of charge'.

From time to time Jaruzelski leaves his office and appears in court to answer the charges against him – 400 pages of them – arising from the 1970 shootings. The two advocates appearing in his defence are, like him, in their seventies. The most recent hearing was postponed 'for health reasons', though the general appears to be in excellent shape.

In the courtroom Jaruzelski suffers and becomes still more gloomy and withdrawn. He brightens up only when someone, maybe there to attend another case, approaches him and shakes his hand. The events of 1970 are now past and forgotten; as for the introduction of martial law in 1981, not everyone in Poland views it negatively. There are those who believe that the alternative was chaos, blood on the streets, violence perpetrated by foreigners, by the soldiers of the Red Army.

'If it weren't for the support I receive from the ordinary people I would have ended my life by now,' says the general in a matter-of-fact way, as if this were an everyday, almost self-evident, decision.

The thought must have been in his mind for a long time. At least since December 1981, in the panic-filled days before the declaration of martial law. The Communist leadership was divided: its representatives knew that they were about to lose their jobs or their honour, or both. One day Jaruzelski invited the Polish president, Henryk Jablonski (more a figurehead than a powerful politician) to join him on the balcony outside the office he occupied as premier. 'If martial law fails and the Russians intervene, you know what we will do, don't you?' he asked. And mimed the act of putting a pistol to his head. The tacit implication was that a patriot who brings dishonour upon his own country by allowing it to be violated by foreigners has only one option: suicide. Though it just might have been a trick to encourage Jaboski to 'sacrifice himself' for the sake of public opinion.

The days leading up to the proclamation of what the Poles call *stan wojenny*, 'a state of war', have long been a subject of dispute among historians, former KGB agents and former Soviet and Polish politicians. Anatoly Gribkov, a retired Red Army general who was joint chief of staff of the armed forces of the Warsaw Pact in 1981, maintains that it was Jaruzelski himself who requested the intervention of Russian troops, fearing that he would be unable to impose martial law without help. Gribkov further maintains that the Politburo in Moscow decided against invasion, and that this upset Jaruzelski, who accused the comrades in Moscow of 'betraying an old friendship'.

The general's response is that, on the contrary, he requested the Politburo not to intervene, and its decision to refrain from sending tanks into Warsaw was a reluctant acceptance of his request.

An endless comedy of errors is being acted out here, each side accusing the other of having got the wrong end of the stick. General Vitaly Pavlov, representative of the KGB in Warsaw from 1973 to 1984, maintains that on 12 December – the day before the proclamation – Jaruzelski telephoned Mikhail Suslov asking for 'direct military assistance', but was refused. General Czeslaw Kiszczak, then the Polish minister for internal affairs, also remembers that phone-call and says that Jaruzelski tried to call Leonid Brezhnev, but Brezhnev refused to speak to him. He spoke to Suslov instead. And Suslov reiterated his refusal, saying that 'in no circumstances' would the Soviets send in troops.

'That was the reassurance I sought, not the reply I feared,' insists Jaruzelski. A fit of anger shakes him. His face becomes even paler.

Having suffered from the sanctions imposed by Western powers as a result of the invasion of Afghanistan in 1979, Moscow was in no mood to risk another diplomatic debacle. Or so it is asserted by one school of thought. In Poland many are convinced that, for all their pressure, the Soviets were just bluffing and would not have dared to send in troops. Moscow was hoping that the Polish comrades would do the job themselves.

Newly discovered documents recording his conversations with the Kremlin show that Jaruzelski was in a state of great mental distress because he was not sure he would be able to cope with the situation alone. Poland's former joint chief of staff, General Florian Siwicki, maintains that Jaruzelski sent him to Moscow in early December to ask for 'a statement demonstrating that the Polish Communists do not stand alone'. But he adds that Moscow refused to sign the document drawn up in Warsaw, which referred to 'fulfilment of the obligations of the alliance' and 'total support for the Polish people in their struggle against counter-revolutionaries'. Siwicki asserts that when he returned to Warsaw empty-handed, a deeply disturbed Jaruzelski commented, 'Our allies have abandoned us' and 'we have exhausted the options available to us'.

'If I said that, I meant it in a negative sense, not because I welcomed the fact that our options were exhausted. And besides, what do you think of this? Does it not prove that these are all lies?' With a quick movement of his hand, the general whips off the dark glasses that protect his delicate sight and replaces them with clear reading glasses. Then, from a leather briefcase, he pulls out a photocopy of a pencil drawing showing tanks and troops on an imaginary battlefront, with the city of Warsaw at its centre. 'I submitted this Soviet drawing to the Polish parliament when it was investigating me. It illustrates how a military intervention by Soviet troops already stationed in Poland, and those sent expressly for the purpose, would have progressed. To say nothing of the preparations being made throughout the Eastern bloc. The Czechoslovakian troops had been issued with gas masks. The East Germans, very critical of any reform, were ready to intervene despite the likelihood of negative repercussions on public opinion that the sight of German troops on Polish soil would have aroused. The instances you have quoted are all lies. I have documents to prove it. And in case you are still not convinced, I will read you the letter Gorbachev wrote on this subject to the Polish parliament when it was investigating me and which he later published in his memoirs, *Life and Works*. It's in chapter twenty-three. Have you read it?'

Jaruzelski's secretary, who has been with him since he moved into the Belvedere (the official residence of the Polish president) on taking office in 1985, knocks on the door. 'May I remind you of that appointment?' Jaruzelski purses his lips. 'Come back tomorrow. I must read you Gorbachev's letter. It is – how shall I describe it? – very revealing. Without it you cannot begin to understand the events of 13 December 1981.'

The following day it is still snowing and the temperature has fallen to −18°C. 'How are you today, General?'

He looks at me. 'There's an old Russian saying.' I expect some exotic Siberian witticism, or a maxim with a Muscovite slant. But no. 'I'm well, as well as can be expected at my age.'

In fact, exactly the same sentiment is expressed in Italian and many other languages. The general looks at me in astonishment, with that expression of supercilious disapproval that the Poles came to recognise as peculiarly his.

'If you say so. However, we had got to Gorbachev's letter, isn't that so? I will translate it very precisely. It is dated 31 August 1995. It is signed by Gorbachev.

As a member of the Soviet Union's Politburo and of the Soviet Communist Party's Central Committee, it was evident to me that General Jaruzelski, First Secretary of the Central Committee of the Polish party, had recourse to every measure available to him to enable Poland to solve peaceably the socio-political crisis into which it had fallen, and that he sought to exclude any use of the armed forces of the Warsaw Pact countries or their interference in the internal affairs of Poland. It is apparent to any unprejudiced person that the introduction of martial law in Poland was the consequence of the internal situation and of an increasingly tense socio-political crisis, as well as the increasing tension in relations between Poland and the Soviet Union. In this situation General Jaruzelski was forced to take the measures he did, accepting their consequences, which in my opinion at the time represented the lesser evil. Jaruzelski and his ministers were faced with the choice between two possibilities both of which were negative and best avoided. And he was desperately searching for a solution to this dilemma. Either accept chaos in Poland, which would have carried with it the risk of the complete collapse of the east European Socialist bloc, or react with force to the events in Poland. Both solutions were unacceptable. His decision was inevitable.'

Gorbachev's letter deals with the matter of the 'lesser evil', though not that of the putative request for military intervention. But the general is agitated, has even become red in the face, and I decide on a less direct line of approach. Why on earth, I ask, did the head of the KGB in Poland say that the request for military assistance came from him, Jaruzelski, because he feared that martial law would be unsustainable without help from abroad?

Jaruzelski again registers impatience. 'If you must take Pavlov's word as gospel . . . then I cannot defend myself. Pavlov invariably repeats what was said at a meeting of the Politburo and later quoted by the dissident Bukowski as well. I wrote a book to refute these statements. When it was dominated by members of Solidarity, our own Polish parliament reopened the question. Bukowski's theory was rejected. Look, these theories appeared in the Polish newspapers with much supporting evidence at precisely the moment when Poland was expressing an interest in joining NATO. They were conceived in order to damage Poland. Up to that moment several Russian generals, such as the Soviet chief of staff General Dobrinin, had been saying that plans were ready for invading Poland. I say this not with any anti-Russian or anti-Soviet subtext, but recognising that this was the logical consequence of the way the world was divided at the time. Considering Poland's geographical and strategic position, there was no alternative.'

But was he never worried that martial law could collapse? That outside military assistance might really be needed to underpin it?

'I had a very clear view of the situation. On 28 October there had been a strike that was only half successful. The numbers taking part were much lower than expected. The results of an opinion poll designed to gauge the relative popularity of various institutions in Poland – from the Church to the army – taken in November 1981 gave the highest number of votes to the army. Ninety three per cent. After the introduction of martial law, out of eight thousand Polish companies only 200 went out on strike. And in the companies on strike, only one-third of the employees took part in the protest. In many cases the strike only lasted a day. The sector where it lasted longest was the miners, where it went on for ten days. Then a disaster in one of the mines, in which many lost their lives, put an end to the strike.'

The general's monologue continues. I try to interrupt him; he notices, but carries on regardless. What I want to say is that if he was so sure of public support, surely there was no need to traumatise the country with tanks and police strong-arm tactics.

Like a wily barrister who has spent many hours sifting defence counsel's argument for possible contradictions, he pre-empts me by a whisker. 'Your logical question at this point should be this: If you were so sure about the stability of the system and the consensus you enjoyed and the weakness of Solidarity, why was it necessary to introduce martial law? I can answer that. You see, the influence of Solidarity was diminishing in Poland at large, but within Solidarity itself the influence of its most radical wing, which was opposed to any dialogue with the government, was gaining strength. On 17 December 1981, the streets of Warsaw and other Polish cities could have seen a rerun of Budapest 1956. I say again: I had no choice.'

Jaruzelski dislikes being called 'Mr President'. 'I prefer the title of General. I still feel like a soldier. In fact, if I have to admit to an error in my life, it is having allowed myself to be persuaded to abandon my military career in favour of politics, first as defence minister, then as prime minister and finally as president.' This is his only self-criticism. All the other so-called faults are categorised as 'lesser evils' for which historical circumstances were to blame. Not once does he say that he believes in democracy or acknowledge that his authoritarian Communist regime was wrong.

Yes, Jaruzelski is right: he was a general, not a president.

'I would like to return to the subject of my family and the origins of my love for the Russians. I am convinced that the attitudes of my mother and sister towards the Russians underwent a change when they came into contact in Siberia with the ordinary Russian "man in the street". Let's be honest: the pathology of the system and that of the ordinary people are two different things. Both my mother and sister watched me striking out on this new path with a degree of understanding, even though they found it difficult to justify. I remember that soon after I returned to Poland at the end of the war, when they were still in Siberia waiting for permission to come home, I wrote them a letter. I told them that there were many things in the new Poland that I neither understood nor liked. But I also said that I had decided to serve Poland as she really was, not Poland as we would have wished her to be. I said that we would have to be prepared to make sacrifices for the real Poland. The only possible Poland. The only actual Poland. We could not change her history or her geography. I chose reality. That of Yalta, if you think of it, apart from anything else. The same reality that had been accepted by the West. So if you blame me, you have to blame yourselves too. And ever since then I have held faithfully to this principle: to serve the Poland that is possible, not the Poland of our dreams.

'You see, the history of Poland is studded with acts of tragic heroism. With romantic attitudes. With fine gestures. Honoré de Balzac, who knew the soul of our people very well having married a Polish woman, wrote in *La Cousine Bette* that if you stand a Pole on the edge of a ravine, he'll throw himself over it. A noble gesture, but one that usually carries a very high price. I found myself on the edge of a ravine, but I made the realistic choice of not throwing myself over it, of not making a fine gesture with inevitable tragic consequences.

'My mother died in 1966. My sister is still alive; she has children who are studying at the Catholic University of Lublin. Her husband is a retired professor who used to lecture at Lublin University, the same university that the Pope attended and at which he taught. My sister and brother-in-law are deeply religious. As was my mother. I too was a believer to begin with, but I gradually grew away from the Church through a long process of change. That does not affect my respect for the Church and, above all, for its role in the history of Poland. I have enormous respect for the moral teachings of the Church. And for the Gospels, naturally. But I don't believe in God.

'A few weeks ago I had an audience with the Holy Father in Rome. And I quoted to him the words of a great Polish writer, Stefan Wilkanowic. "The hearts of the Polish people are very close to the Pope, and their heads are far from him." The Poles love the Pope, but they do not necessarily obey his teaching. I'm not a Roman Catholic, yet I should like to see the Poles give much greater heed than they do to the Pope's teachings.

'I admit that this was not exactly how I thought on the day Karol Wojtyla was elected. Like all the other Polish leaders of the day, I had conflicting emotions. On one side was the satisfaction, the pride of having a Pole on the throne of Peter. And the hope that this would help the international standing of our country. On the other hand we were worried that the election of Wojtyla would increase the influence of the Roman Catholic Church in Poland, making it a yet more problematic partner for the ruling power. With hindsight, that concern was unfounded. Successive contacts have shown me that not only does the Pope have a very clear understanding of what is happening in Poland, but he sees it in relation to what is happening in the rest of the world. He saw the faults of the system that prevailed in Poland, but is also critical of the state of affairs elsewhere, in the capitalist world for a start.

'Yes, I know, the Polish government certainly dragged its feet before giving permission for Wojtyla to visit the country. The first visit was in 1979. At the time I was defence minister and not responsible for political decisions such as this. I well remember how worried we were that enthusiasm for the Pope's visit would get out of hand and create a situation beyond our control. The visit was risky. I was not in charge of the negotiations, but I remember that one of the thorniest points raised concerned the date, which coincided with the feast of St Stanislaus.

'The problem was this. A thousand years ago the king of Poland condemned the bishop of Cracow, Stanislaus Stepanoswski, to death. For a thousand years historians have been divided over the facts of the matter. The supporters of the Church say that St Stanislaus gave his life in defence of the faith. Other historians, serious scholars, say that he was killed for treason against the Polish state.'

Treason?

Stanislaus, like Wojtyla a bishop of Cracow, incurred the enmity of King Boleslaus the Bold when he denounced his cruelties and injustices. Stanislaus excommunicated the king and halted services in the cathedral when Boleslaus entered. So Boleslaus himself killed the bishop while he was saying mass. Since then Stanislaus has been the symbol of Polish nationhood. And what I think this well-educated, aristocratic, gentlemanly general is trying to say is that Boleslaus might have had just cause for killing him. For 'treason against the Polish state', for disobeying the ruling authority, for criticising his sovereign.

Augusto Pinochet would have loved that.

Jaruzelski is unfazed. Maybe the Catholic historians are right about St Stanislaus. Maybe the Communist historians are. He can't be bothered to take sides. He doesn't see the moral issue.

'So you understand why we could reasonably argue that we did not want this thousand-year-old quarrel to resurface when the situation in Poland was already difficult enough. It was unnecessary.

'When the Pope was elected in 1978, no one could have imagined that only thirteen years later the Soviet Union would have ceased to exist and the political system of the Socialist countries would have come to an end. So we were slightly concerned, but not really worried. Let's say that the anxieties raised by the election of the first Polish Pope were – to use military terminology – more tactical than strategic.

'The attempted assassination of Pope Wojtyla came as a surprise. I had been prime minister for exactly three months. Here in Poland we knew only what we read in the international press, including the information about the so-called "Bulgarian connection". Later, during a Warsaw Pact summit, I asked the Bulgarian leader Todor Zhivkov for his response to such rumours. He replied, "General Jaruzelski, do you really think that if we had set up an operation of that kind, we would have left that chap Sergei Ivanov, the Rome representative of Bulgarian Airlines, to be interrogated by the West's secret services?" Since 11 September we have seen how diverse the roots of terrorism can be, to how many forms of fanaticism they can be connected. I've been told that Ali Agca, who was recently moved to a new prison in Turkey, has now changed his story about the attempted assassination of the Pope. He no longer refers to any Bulgarian connection.

'Another historical mystery is that of the Katyn forest graves. Yes, we now know that the twenty-two thousand Polish prisoners of war killed and buried there and at other sites nearby, officers representing a large part of the Polish governing and middle class, were massacred by the Russians with a bullet in the back of the neck. But it was originally thought that the Nazis were responsible. I myself have seen the statements of people on the spot who said it was the Germans. Then doubts started to be voiced. We heard Radio Free Europe raise this question several times and insist on the guilt of Moscow. To begin with, we in Warsaw wrote off these accusations as typical Cold War propaganda. But with the passage of time our demands that Moscow provide proof of Nazi responsibility became more insistent. "Comrades," I said to my colleagues in Moscow, "we naturally believe what you say. But give us the ammunition we need to refute this propaganda from the West." They replied that the accusations against Soviet troops were capitalist provocation that deserved to be ignored. The silence lasted until Gorbachev's time.

'Throughout that period I was one of those who, by then, realised where the truth lay but maintained that to attack Moscow over the matter of the Katyn mass graves would be a useless exercise. We could not bring the victims back to life and we would damage the bilateral relationship. But at a certain point I felt the moment had come to reopen this chapter of history.'

By then the Berlin Wall was already demolished. Communism had been defeated. The Cold War was over. The truth about Katyn had been revealed in a number of books. The general's conversion had come a little late. But he loves to think of himself as a courageous reformist.

'Even Gorbachev was still not sure. He was worried about the reaction of the military establishment. And I understood that. No one knew better than me the kind of resistance the military could offer to any suggestion of reform. But on the eve of my visit to Moscow in April 1990 I made it clear to the Russians that I would go only if the Kremlin made an unequivocal admission of responsibility. And Gorbachev admitted that Katyn was a Soviet, not a Nazi, crime. Even where Katyn is concerned, my role has been underrated, I have not been treated fairly. All the credit has gone to Lech Walesa and Boris Yeltsin who, years later, revealed the existence of a document signed by Stalin ordering the killing of the Poles. But no one ever remembers that it was I who forced Moscow's hand. I, who was accused by the West of being a hard-nosed, intransigent politician.

'The history of relations between the West and the Soviet bloc is full of paradoxes. Gorbachev told me personally – and he also mentions it in his book – that after the failed coup orchestrated by anti-reformist hard-liners, he received telephone calls, some from George Bush, some even from Lech Walesa, expressing support. But they also asked him to stand firm, to preserve – even to strengthen – the Soviet Union, because the West needed it. Our former enemies were terrified by the idea of losing the USSR, which until quite recently they had called "the empire of evil".'

It was more difficult for the Poles to swallow martial law ideologically than to deal with it in daily life. Solidarity, though outlawed, was still as strong as ever. On the streets people continued to tell jokes against the regime. The curfew, far from being enforced in Soviet fashion, was treated with the disorganised tolerance, the casual, laid-back approach which the Polish people share with southern Europeans.

Jerzy Kisielewski, journalist son of a famous Polish dissident writer, tells the following story: 'I remember an occasion when, returning home after a day working on the newspaper, I got into a taxi and the driver, without so much as looking at my face, went on listening to the radio as he drove. I started to listen too, rather abstractedly. I noticed something wrong, then realised what it was. The driver was tuned into Radio Free Europe, owned by the American government and transmitted from Monaco. Absolutely forbidden officially. The driver had no idea who I was, I could easily have been a plain-clothes policeman. But he wasn't worried. Everyone knew that the risks – terrible in theory – were negligible in practice.'

Intellectuals sometimes invited arrest deliberately in order to boost their anti-Jaruzelski credentials. Sometimes an arrest on the orders of the armed forces was challenged by the police who, from having been a 'revolutionary militia', had now become simply the professional guardian of law and order and a bitter rival of the army. Erich Honecker, the extremely hard-line leader of East Germany, protested from his palace of Pankow in East Berlin, 'Our Polish comrades are not doing enough to repress criminals. If they need assistance from us, we are willing to lend them a hand.'

In Warsaw this is a Christmas of economic crisis. Workers are being laid off. The growth of the last few years has come to a halt. Foreign investment has dried up because labour costs – entirely due to the contracts wrested from employers by Solidarity in the Eighties – are the highest in Eastern Europe.

In General Jaruzelski's office, at eleven o'clock in the morning, his two bodyguards and the secretary down small shots of vodka. A modest celebration compared to other offices, where employees will be treated to a meal in a restaurant. As soon as a visitor appears, the vodka bottles are hidden – with embarrassed smiles – beneath the plastic chairs.

Snow now covers everything. Even the Palace of Culture looks less ominous beneath its thick white blanket.

'I'm told you have met Colonel Mengistu. I remember him well as a young Ethiopian leader. He visited Warsaw in 1979 and seemed pleased with everything he saw. He told me he wanted to end feudalism in Ethiopia and replace it with our brand of Socialism. Of course, he said nothing about how he intended to achieve this objective . . . They tell me he is going to be tried for crimes against humanity, but we'll have to see on what basis these charges are prepared. I'm thinking of the trial that resulted in a prison sentence for my friend Egon Krenz, the last East German head of state.'

General, Mengistu says that he was betrayed by his friend Gorbachev.

'He is not the only one to say that. There are many others. But what could Gorbachev do? He also had to govern the real and realisable Soviet Union, not the ideal one.'

Nevertheless, he presided over the break-up of the Soviet Union. What does Gorbachev represent for you? A hero or a traitor?

'Gorbachev is a great man. A man who, although he did not start out to be a reformer, ended by changing the world. There was a great river, the river of history, whose waters were dammed behind a rock, or rather an enormous block of stone. Gorbachev was the man who lifted away the stone and allowed the waters to run free. Then, to me personally, Gorbachev remains a dear friend.'

And the Pope?

Jaruzelski's expression becomes serious. He heaves a deep sigh.

'An enormous personality, a great intellectual, a great Polish patriot, but at the same time a true citizen of the world. I have had eight audiences with him and can say that, while hundreds of millions of people in the world know how good he is at speaking to the masses, far fewer know how good he is at listening. You know, I have met many statesmen and leaders who, at a certain point in their lives, became capable only of monologues. The Pope, on the other hand, knows how to listen. And he has always listened to my arguments, my problems.'

Lech Walesa?

'Ah, Lech.' The general smiles. He well knows that the street hero of Solidarity, the freedom fighter with a Holy Mary badge always clipped to the lapel of his cheap jacket and ten million supporters behind him, is now irrelevant, if not disgraced. A companion in misfortune, in a way. 'Lech, an extraordinary man, gifted with a great natural instinct for politics, though unfortunately without the intellectual, cultural or personal qualifications to lead a country like Poland. But he got it right very often, he knew where he was going. My discussions with Lech have always been open and honest – and often . . . amusing, too.'

Marshal Tito?

'I met him three times. Twice during his lifetime and then at his funeral. He once even invited me to join him for a short cruise on his private yacht in the Adriatic. On all three occasions – including the funeral – yes, I thought of him as a very intelligent man, who had successfully held the Yugoslav republics together and managed to oppose Stalin without disastrous consequences to his country. But over the years his style had tended to become monarchical, almost that of a Byzantine prince besotted with wealth and luxury. And this tendency was encouraged by the West.'

Fidel Castro?

'At the beginning we were all dazzled by Fidel. Including you Westerners. A fascinating, charismatic man. A man who could establish an immediate rapport with any crowd. And I am quite capable of distinguishing between the artificial mass hysteria generated by the propaganda machine and the real thing. In my position I've . . . let's say studied these matters from very close quarters.' He has the grace to smile at this point. 'Fidel was an extremely capable and good man. Then times changed and he was unable to change with them. He has always been consistent, true to himself. He could not move ahead as we in Poland have done. He became fixed in his ideas. I also know his brother, Raul, very well. A good chap, but not in the same league as Fidel. Who knows what will happen to Cuba after Castro . . .'

Ronald Reagan?

'Mmm . . . My feelings about Reagan have been completely different at different times. At the beginning my opinion of him was decidedly negative. The sanctions he imposed on Poland after martial law were very painful. And for me, Reagan was simply a hypocrite. He received the Romanian dictator Ceaucescu, who had been operating martial law for twenty years, with full honours, yet it took him only a few hours to decree an embargo against us when we were in the difficult position of having to declare a state of war. Later I changed my opinion. And when I saw him standing beside Gorbachev in Red Square saying, with a big smile on his face, that the empire of evil no longer existed, then I started to see him as a man capable of changing his mind. And I admired him for it. His vice-president, George Bush, made a very favourable impression on me when he visited Warsaw.'

What about Helmut Kohl?

'He's another man I kept at arm's length to begin with. An extremely long arm's length, to be honest. Yet Kohl has done a great deal for Europe. And I'm sorry that his political career ended so dishonourably.'

And Erich Honecker?

'It would be easy to dismiss him as an unexciting personality, a grey-suited bureaucrat. And of course he ruled East Germany with an iron fist. He was a dogmatist. But I also saw a dynamic side to the man. First and foremost, I never saw him without remembering that he spent ten years in a Nazi prison, an experience that left him deeply scarred. But he was no fanatic. He was, for instance, extremely keen on physical fitness and exercise. One day, after a political meeting, he even gave me a special oxygen machine, made by his scientists, which was supposed to regenerate the skin and increase one's sense of physical well-being. Although sceptical, I took it home. But when I used it I began to feel the benefit. Honecker was like his machine: you could be sceptical about him at the beginning, but put to the proof, he did not disappoint.'

Now it's December 2001, exactly twenty years since he appeared on television, in uniform and against the background of Poland's red-and-white flag with the Polish eagle in the middle, to make his announcement in a hard, dry voice. Twenty years since what was, in fact, the real coup d'état.

Today, as I prepare to leave Warsaw, the snow has stopped falling. Girls and boys with knapsacks on their backs cluster around the station McDonald's. They are university students on their way home to the rural vastnesses of provincial Poland for the Christmas vacation.

Jaruzelski, too, is about to leave Warsaw for his dacha surrounded by snow-laden birches that remind him of his childhood in Siberia. He has called me to his office to say goodbye. But I am also here to be reproached. 'You are putting me in a book together with all the criminals of our time. The only one missing is Pol Pot.' I see the ghost of a wistful smile. 'But you have not asked me a single question about the subject which, from my point of view, constitutes the principal regret of my career.'

I remember St Stanislaus and his modern version, Father Popieluszko. Maybe the general is about to tell me that he identifies with King Boleslaus. Both bald and both authoritarian. Both believers in realpolitik more than in ideals. 'I'm listening, General. You want to talk about the assassination of Father Popieluszko?'

Jerzy Popieluszko was a popular young priest with a parish in the suburbs of Warsaw, who spoke out against the abuses of Communism and supported Solidarity. Thousands flocked to hear his Sunday sermons. He was abducted on 19 October 1984. His savagely beaten body was found eleven days later in an icy reservoir. The crime shook Poland and, according to the opposition, was carried out on the express orders of the government.

'No, Popieluszko was killed by a crazy fanatic. The man later wrote me a letter apologising for having brought shame on the country. The government was not responsible in any way. Certainly, relations with the Church were difficult; there were constant clashes. But none of us would ever have given the order for a murder like that. No, I am referring to an earlier time, one that many now pretend to have forgotten. I'm talking about 1967–8, when Poland was in the grip of a psychosis that we called "anti-Zionism" but which was, in fact, anti-Semitism. I was then joint chief of staff. I was in a position of responsibility. I could have tried to influence events. But I didn't have the energy – or the courage – to mount an opposition. Anti-Semitic Poland was not the only Poland possible. The chance to fight was there. But I didn't fight. You see, I'm blamed for making many mistakes that I never made. I'm on trial for crimes that I never perpetrated. And I'm absolved of the only real fault for which I should be blamed.

'Life can be such a paradox. They all wanted me to throw myself over the edge of the ravine. To make the fine gesture. To be theatrical. But I've never been an actor. I've lived in the real world. Now I have to go. My wife is waiting for me. Have a happy new year. And be fair to me. Ask yourself what you would have done if you were in my shoes. No, in my military boots.'

Hoxha

A pyramid is power. It is repression, force, and wealth. But it is just as much domination of the rabble; the narrowing of its minds; the weakening of its will; monotony; and waste. O my Pharaoh, it is your most reliable guardian. Your secret police. Your army. Your fleet. Your harem. The higher it is, the tinier your subjects will seem. And the smaller your subjects, the more you rise.

from *The Pyramid* by Ismail Kadare

When I first entered her cell, the only thing I could see was the mattress. It lay on the bare stone floor with neither sheet nor pillow. After a while, I made out two piles of books lying beside it, thick tomes in good-quality bindings with French titles. Neatly stacked as if on a professor's bedside table. A pair of spectacles lay on the topmost book, magnifying the first words of the title, *Histoire de la philosophie . . .*'

Minutes earlier I had been walking through the sun-drenched streets of Tirana. It was one of those summer days when Orient and Mediterranean meet and the different shades of golden light lend even the unplastered blocks of flats, erected in the Albanian capital by the Chinese in the Seventies, an aura of cheerfulness.

I was looking for the maximum-security prison. Its entrance was at the end of a narrow street flooded by a burst water-main. The heavy gate was surrounded by a crowd jostling to gain entry. Men in singlets and flip-flops were hammering on the iron grille and shouting angrily. Perspiring women sat in old, rusty Alfa Romeos with Italian number-plates parked in the middle of the street. All were relatives of people arrested the previous night during one of the frequent trawls carried out on the orders of the new president, cardiologist-turned-politician Sali Berisha. As the pro-Berisha press explained every day, the intention of these police raids was 'to bring to trial and punish those responsible for five decades of dictatorship' and, in the meanwhile, to teach the population about the marvels of democracy.

Every now and then a guard appeared outside the main gate of the prison, glanced at the crowd, spat on the ground and, with an air of total indifference, disappeared again, shutting the door behind him. The only people allowed through were the warders arriving for the next shift, crammed into an old blue van discarded by the Italian police and donated to the Albanian government. It still bore the insignia of the *carabinieri*.

The prison governor received me in a room with closed shutters and walls painted the same green as Fascist-era classrooms in Italy. After glancing rapidly at the document authorising an interview with one of his inmates, freshly rubber-stamped by a judge, he hastily shut it away in a drawer as if physical contact with the piece of paper was offensive to him. Or dangerous. Then he dismissed me.

The prison corridors were full of more men in singlets. Prisoners, perhaps, or policemen, or possibly men who had just swapped one role for the other and were still wondering in which category they really belonged. Not even Angela Rapiki and her husband Albert were always able to tell cops and robbers apart.

Angela was a reporter working for ATA, the official press agency, until recently the mouthpiece of the Albanian Stalinist regime. Albert had recently been appointed to the new, reformed Foreign Office and was hoping to be posted abroad, possibly to Malta. I had met them by chance and they had offered to help, maybe because in those days a foreigner was still a rarity in Tirana and they were eager to spend some time with strangers from abroad.

Our first problem was to find someone to authorise the interview. This was not going to be easy because few highly placed officials would look favourably on such an unusual application. Together we sifted through the names of personal friends and political contacts, family connections and rival clans. Then Angela and Albert decided that our best bet would be to visit Tirana's ministries and law courts, looking for a legal loophole that would sanction the interview. Ministries and tribunals were all located in the same street, all built of red brick in the style favoured by Mussolini during the Fascist occupation of Albania, all with petitioners camped on the stairways and all equipped with ancient black typewriters.

Eventually a judge who was an old schoolmate of Angela's interrupted a trial – a murder case resulting from some long-running provincial feud – and, without asking me a single question, signed the permit on a sheet of brown paper. Then he resumed his trial, ordering the family of the victim and the family of the suspect to stop chatting amicably to each other and to take their seats.

I was thrilled and considerably surprised. This amused Angela. 'You didn't know?' she asked me. 'Personal favours are the only merchandise that has always been in abundant supply in Albania, even during the worst days of the dictatorship.'

On our way to the prison, Angela became increasingly nervous. She would not tell me why. But when the gate was locked behind us, her face went white. She admitted that she wasn't up to meeting 'that woman'. All of a sudden the very idea of facing the flesh-and-blood reality of the incubus that had dominated her life was too much for her.

'You simply can't imagine the horror we Albanians feel at the mere mention of that name. You can't imagine the fear it triggers. It's as if she and her husband, over fifty years of dictatorship, had actually convinced us that they were superhuman. And they tell us that she is still disdainful, that her eyes are still cold and piercing. I don't think I'm strong enough to meet the eyes of our Lady Macbeth.'

I persuaded Angela to think again. Finally she took a deep breath, like an athlete before a race, and agreed. Yes, she too would face the Black Widow.

So, after the brief meeting with the prison governor, Albert,

Angela and I raced up the prison stairs together. At the top we were met by our escort, two soldiers, unshaven and with the pronounced cheekbones of the Albanian peasant. They wore their blue uniforms unbuttoned and carried heavy rifles of Second World War vintage slung over their shoulders.

As we were walking down a crowded corridor, it was Albert's turn to blench. He tugged at my arm. 'You didn't notice,' he said quietly, glancing over his shoulder, 'but one of the prisoners, a former Communist leader, has just scared the hell out of me. He said, "Watch your step, because when we're back in power we'll have our revenge."'

I could find no words of reassurance.

After climbing more stairs, we stopped in front of a cell. The guards gestured to us to go in, but neither dared touch the iron door, which was unlocked. The Black Widow was in there.

We all hesitated. No one – not the judge, not the prison governor, not even Angela or her husband – had mentioned her name. Everyone was scared by it. Besides, there was no need.

Since the Black Widow and her husband had first come to power half a century earlier, their name had been indissolubly associated with Albania itself. Everything revolved around the quasi-sacred name of the Great Leader and his spouse. But this did not imply that it could be freely spoken. The regime founded by this remarkable couple was so concerned by its possible misuse that, to avoid it being profaned, they had even made its utterance unlawful except on official occasions or by authorised officials. Paradoxically, under the new government of Dr Sali Berisha the situation was unchanged, but for the opposite reason. Political chaos and economic decline were now so rife that they were afraid the hated name might induce nostalgia. Or deference. So even in the new and 'democratic' Tirana it was still inadvisable to allow the name to pass your lips. Possibly forbidden. Certainly dangerous.

To Angela's horror, I finally pushed open the door and said, '*Buongiorno*, Mrs Hoxha.'

★   ★   ★

They came to arrest me three days later. When I returned from supper at an open-air café with John Battelle, an American aid worker, they were waiting for me in the hall of the dingy old Hotel Tirana. There were three of them, in uniforms identical to the prison warders' except that the buttons were done up. And they had shaved. They accosted me as I went to retrieve the key to my room. 'Just a check-up. You must come with us. It won't take long. It's only a formality,' said the soldiers in Italian learned from the television.

Ilir, the concierge who had known me for a week and eavesdropped on my calls, was on the phone. I heard him say, 'No, he's not here. Not here' and guessed – correctly – that he was speaking to my wife, Pia, calling from Italy at the time we had previously arranged. There was nothing I could do about it. His voice trembled as he added, in a whisper, '*Signora*, the police are here . . . Police . . . Sigurimi.' The hated secret service.

At the sight of the welcoming party, John paled. It was his first encounter with hostile police officers in this country to which Washington, only a few days before, had sent him 'to help the new, emerging democracy'. We had met a couple of days before and had decided to meet up in the evenings to chat about his Italian grandparents and exchange views and ideas.

Thinking quickly, I said, 'John, run to the Italian Embassy and tell them that I'm being arrested. Please.' He smiled and sped off in his all-American shorts, leaving me alone with the policemen.

It was dark by then. Outside the hotel on Skanderbeg Square – a white cube furnished with pieces from the Fifties and posters advertising a mysterious national tourist board that existed in name only – another Fiat van in the livery of the Italian *carabinieri* was waiting. We crossed the square just as the people of Tirana emerged, as they always do, for their evening walk. Men were lighting up Partizani cigarettes, extracting them from packets still bearing the Communist red star; many were holding hands, as is customary throughout the lands that were once provinces of the great Ottoman Empire. Girls were strolling along languidly, ignoring the wolf-whistles that followed them.

Months later John told me the story of what happened to him next.

Finding the embassy already closed for the night, he knocked on the door of the ambassador's residence, a few blocks away. The ambassador was hosting a formal dinner party. Black tie. Not shorts. So once John had delivered his message, he was briskly thanked and whisked off to the kitchen for refreshments. He was not immediately impressed, expecting to be repaid with a warmer welcome and possibly an invitation to join the party. But only a few minutes later he was thanking his lucky stars for the ambassador's sense of decorum: the very attractive daughter of the house, herself taking refuge in the kitchen from the formal party upstairs, fell in love with him on the spot. The very next day they were on holiday together on some Italian beach on the other side of the Adriatic.

While John was enjoying himself in the ambassador's kitchen, I was being locked into a cell at Police Station Number One. My passport had been confiscated. The cell was dark, but I could see that someone had smeared the wall with a bloodied hand, leaving a sinister palm-print. From the corner of the cell, a boy in uniform with the flashes torn off asked me, 'What did you do to get thrown in here?' Feeling like an actor in a B-movie, I replied, 'I don't know. There must be some mistake. I'm innocent. And what about you, what did you do?'

He had the pale face of a child who has been crying and wants to go home, to some farm in the north, away from a world he doesn't understand and which doesn't understand him. His rudimentary chronicle encapsulated the political confusion of the time, the contradictions of a government democratic in name but still dictatorial in its methods. 'They took us to the main square where there was going to be a demonstration. They told us, the soldiers, to aim at the heads of the crowd. I obeyed. One person died. They arrested me for murder. They said they never gave the order.'

I put my hand on his shoulder and lied. 'So you are innocent too. Don't worry, everything will be okay.'

Three days earlier, in her cell on the second floor of the maximum-security prison, Nexhmije Hoxha had used almost the same words. 'I'm innocent. They are mistaken. I wanted nothing but the well-being of my country.'

The entire floor was occupied by former leaders of the old regime. Many had fought as partisans in the Second World War. A generation of beings above the law, who had obsessively plastered every wall in the country with slogans such as 'Praise and glory to the Communist Party of Albania', 'Thank you Enver, Long Live Enver', 'The Albanian people will not sell itself for roubles or dollars, but believes passionately in proletarian internationalism'. Obstinate hard-liners who had kept the cult of Stalin alive until the end of the Eighties, still busily erecting new busts of Uncle Joe in front of schools and factories when in the rest of Eastern Europe those of Lenin had already been thrown out.

The last time I had seen these hard-liners, the same people who were sharing the prison floor with Nexhmije Hoxha were still in power. It was at the May Day ceremonies in 1989, the last Stalinist May Day in Europe.

They arrived − after a short drive through the only capital city in the world where ordinary people were forbidden to own cars and where there were no traffic lights − in a fleet of black Volvos with the curtains closed. Septuagenarians with big red badges on their crumpled jackets, holding a clenched fist to their temples, their inscrutable gaze hidden behind sunglasses while their lips shaped the words of popular songs celebrating the partisan feats of Enver and Nexhmije Hoxha during the war against the German Nazis and Italian Fascists.

The *Nomenklatura* had remained faithful to the Hoxhas for nearly fifty years. When Enver, acting on Nexhmije's advice, froze Albania into a rigidly autarchic economy and broke off relations with Moscow in 1961 and with Peking in 1978, he accused both of not being sufficiently committed to Marxist ideals. The old guard had stayed loyal despite the Hoxhas revising Article No. 28 of the Constitution so that it forbade any relations whatsoever with both 'imperialist and revisionist countries', plunging Albania into complete political isolation.

In the Seventies Enver became ill. A double – the dentist Petar Shapallo, literally taken hostage by the government and kept hidden even from his own family – was required to take his place ever more often at long official ceremonies. He lived with the Hoxhas. Nexhmije was now in power and pressing for a hard line with a moralistic bias. It was she (or so they say) who ordered customs officials to shave off the beards and moustaches of the few foreigners allowed to enter the country.

At a certain point the dictatorship became more violent, more self-obsessed. Thousands of streets and city squares were renamed '8 November' in honour of the day on which the Albanian Communist Party was founded. In 1967 religion was outlawed and Albania became the first nation in the world to be officially atheist, its churches and mosques razed to the ground.

But monuments of a different type were about to be erected, more robust temples dedicated to the true religion of the Hoxhas: the stubborn Albanian spirit. It was Comrade Enver who conceived the idea of installing concrete bunkers built like tanks. Unlike real tanks, Hoxha's were immovable – but they were immensely cheaper to manufacture so their final number became huge: 700,000, one for every four inhabitants. Little pyramids that, like the Great Pyramid of Cheops, served more than one purpose.

Their construction absorbed the energies of the population, emptied the state treasuries so avoiding the slightest risk of any distribution of wealth, and signalled that the country of the *shqiptarë,* the 'sons of eagles', was surrounded by enemies intent on invading it. As Enver declared just before his death in 1985, (the same year that a young technocrat called Mikhail Gorbachev was elected secretary-general of the Soviet Communist Party and a moustached electrician called Lech Walesa was shaking Communist Poland to its foundations), the Albanians were prepared to 'eat grass' in their bunkers rather than surrender. Or compromise.

So, the Hoxhas and the *Nomenklatura* were innocent. They 'wanted nothing but the well-being of the country'.

As soon as we entered her cell, the Widow rose to her feet and stood beside her mattress like a soldier ready for inspection. At seventy-three the oldest woman prisoner in Europe, she dressed like the principal of a girls' college: navy-blue skirt reaching to below the knee, navy-blue blouse with white spots, and sensible shoes. Her hair was scraped into a bun at the nape of her neck. For half a century this had been the only 'fashion' tolerated in Stalinist Albania. She had worn it to show that not even the Great Leader and his wife had any truck with luxury. And they were still revolutionaries.

Intimidated, Angela could not avoid greeting her deferentially with lowered eyes. Nexhmije Hoxha did not even respond. It was an embarrassing moment. As there were no chairs in the cell, I suggested she sat on the mattress. She refused. It would have been undignified. She replied to my questions in the old-fashioned Italian of a retired schoolteacher, with no trace of an accent, the well-turned phrases clipped and precise. I tried to provoke her. But she remained unflappable.

How did she feel about having nothing now, she who had once had everything, who indeed had once been everything to a whole nation? 'I'm a strong woman,' she replied. 'As a partisan I slept beside Enver in the snow. And when we were fighting the Nazi-Fascists he and I had some bad moments. But afterwards ours was the only country which liberated itself by itself, with no help from the Americans, unlike you Italians or the rest of Europe. I'm still a fighter. Such are the highs and lows in political life, wouldn't you agree?' And she looked at me, her eyes hard with sarcasm.

But, I asked her, you would not equate the Nazi occupation

of Albania with the first attempt in the long history of the country to introduce a multi-party system? The Widow showed not a flicker of emotion. 'On the contrary, there is a direct comparison. You only have to remember the quislings who were defeated by the partisans and emigrated to America after the war. They are now flocking back to Albania to realise their dream of a country in thrall to capitalism. These are the same people that Enver and I defeated on the mountains, in 1944. The traitors who sided with Hitler and Mussolini. Those who tried to invade Albania after the Second World War with the help of mercenaries paid by the British government. The same people Enver and I have been fighting all our lives.'

Nexhmije spoke as if Enver were still alive. As if Communism were still alive. 'I have always been an idealist. I am old and tired now, but prison has not changed my way of thinking. Enver and I will always be true Marxists. We believe in it, we have always believed in it.' She paused and, glancing out of the window as if she could see the office of the hated Sali Berisha, formerly the Hoxha family's doctor, said with disgust, 'Those people believe in nothing, only in dollars.'

Immediately after winning the election, Berisha had accused a dozen or so of the old regime's leaders of corruption and put them in prison. Hoxha's widow was suspected of having bank accounts in Switzerland, villas in Italy, estates in South Africa. The charges that resulted in an eleven-year prison sentence included that of misappropriating the sum of 300 dollars. It had not been possible to establish more.

She denied even that. 'Not a single lek stuck to my fingers. Everything that Enver and I received from the state was spent on official hospitality.' She spoke as if the state and the Hoxhas were separate entities. 'Yes,' she repeated, relishing the phrase, 'official hospitality . . . The foreign dignitaries stayed at our house. International relations were maintained at our expense. Certainly Enver and I lived better than most people, but we worked like slaves to build this country from nothing. We sacrificed our youth, everything, to build a Socialist Albania.

No one before us had ever built schools, hospitals, factories. The country we inherited was still emerging from the Middle Ages, from feudalism. We made it self-sufficient.'

Angela, trying to sound matter-of-fact to disguise her emotion, asked about her legal position. 'I am a political prisoner,' replied Lady Macbeth. 'For twenty-one months this government has deprived me of my liberty with false accusations. This is the second summer I have spent in the heat of this isolation cell, and for the last four weeks they have even forbidden me any contact with my three children.'

For the first time she looked Angela squarely in the eyes, as if she, Angela, were the official representative of the new regime. 'You claim to believe in democracy, but in fact you are counter-revolutionaries acting like dictators. You should be ashamed of yourselves. Write about it, write about the way I am treated by the politicians of this democracy.' The last word came out with the lip-curling disgust of someone swallowing a bitter medicine. Her arms akimbo. Her eyes assuming the hard, piercing look that Angela had so dreaded.

Had she any regrets about ordering the torture and persecution of her opponents? Nexhmije Hoxha's jaw tightened. 'No.' And she repeated it. 'No. Because a state has to defend itself from those who plot against it. Of course, there may have been some excesses . . .' Then she shrugged as if to say, 'Trifles not worth mentioning.'

She did not say whether she included among the excesses her proclamation of the newly created crime of 'subversion, treason and propaganda', an offence so vaguely defined that it was applicable to any act of which she and Enver disapproved. But at the height of the Hoxhas' power, the Sigurimi had no need to hunt for criminals. The 'criminals' hunted each other. Every year each citizen was required to write an autobiographical report and list neighbours, relatives or work colleagues guilty of 'subversion, treason and propaganda'. Those who preferred not to denounce others were allowed to denounce themselves. It was normal for people to disappear into labour camps for years at a time, to be tortured.

She did not mention that it was forbidden to apply for a passport, or to read books such as Boris Pasternak's *Doctor Zhivago* and George Orwell's *Nineteen Eighty-Four*, while the only books studied in school were those written by Enver, which were printed in dozens of foreign languages by a big state-owned printing works.

Nor that news of the *soi-disant* scientific and economic breakthroughs achieved by Albania, 'model nation the envy of the world', was broadcast around the world by Radio Tirana.

Trifles not worth mentioning?

'Perhaps the abolition of religion was excessive,' the Widow finally admitted. 'But Enver had no wish to destroy churches and mosques. It was our Chinese allies, who were the only ones helping us financially and militarily, and the younger members of the Party who forced that on him. Enver and I only wanted Muslims, Orthodox Christians and Catholics to live peaceably side by side. And we were right. We wanted everyone to feel they were just Albanians. And see what is happening now in the Balkans as the result of religious and ethnic conflicts. History will prove us right. Capitalist propaganda described us as backward and introverted. On the contrary, you will come to realise that ours was a modern vision.'

I reminded her of Mother Teresa of Calcutta, the Albanian-born Roman Catholic nun who had made several controversial visits to the 'eagles' nest' under the Hoxhas. Mother Teresa was also a frequent guest of another infamous dynasty, the Duvalier of Haiti. In both cases, the saintly and venerated nun had had only smiles for her hosts, refusing to speak against them or their repressive regimes, one ferociously Stalinist, the other corrupted and capitalist.

'Mother Teresa was a true patriot. A great Albanian,' said the Widow. 'She showed the world how to help the poor and devoted her life to the neediest without interfering in political issues. Just like any religious leader should do. Instead, many of them want to mess with the people's choices. They want political roles. Which is exactly what was happening in Albania before the declaration of atheism. And what they tell me is happening now, with all these Islamic organisations opening up shop in Tirana with nobody able to track their real activities.'

The Widow stopped and looked me straight in the eyes. 'I don't believe in God. I'm a Marxist. I believe in man and in the people. But we liked Mother Teresa. You know, she felt at home here. She came with an open mind and praised our achievements.'

Night had closed in on the cell in Police Station Number One. I was called from my cell and seated in front of an officer, who questioned me from behind a desk straight out of a school classroom. The interrogation opened with the old Stalinist technique of asking the same question ten or twenty times, hoping to catch the subject out in a contradiction. 'We followed you the day you went to a village beyond Fier. We want a list of the names and surnames of everyone you spoke to . . . We know you're not a journalist, but a spy in contact with enemies of the state. Who are you working for?'

First a friendly officer, then an unfriendly one, then the friendly one again.

One of them noticed the little gold cross on a chain round my neck. 'Are you a Christian?' – 'Yes.' They exchanged glances. 'We are all Muslims.' Around three in the morning I decided to force the issue. 'I am a foreign citizen and I have the legal right to contact my embassy. You have no proof that would substantiate any accusation against me. I shall now leave.' I rose and went towards the door. Two soldiers tried to stop me, but I evaded them. At the end of the corridor another soldier released the safety catch on his rifle and levelled the weapon at me. I returned to my chair in front of the officer. As a punishment he tore up the statement. 'Let's begin again from the beginning. Tell me your name, your address and for whom you are really working.'

After another hour, at around four in the morning, they suspended the interrogation. Realising that their Italian was not good enough to carry on, they sent for someone from a nearby block of flats.

He was a little man of about fifty with a scarred face and sad blue eyes. The little man shook my hand and introduced himself as 'Rudolf Carku. Or rather, Rodolfo Carku. I'm Italian, but I was born and grew up in Albania. Are you interested in my story?' – 'Sure,' I said before adding, with a glance at the guards, 'but they might not agree . . .' – 'Don't worry, they will stop us when they are ready to ask you more questions.'

So Rodolfo told me about his life as a 'lost' Italian. 'When the war ended my poor mother, Carolina Comaschi, who is still alive and is at home awaiting my return, was among those who decided to stay on. Of course, we never imagined what was about to happen.'

Rodolfo glanced over his shoulder. 'My poor mother comes from one of the best families in Bologna, the Comaschi. She fell in love with an Albanian and married him despite her family's opposition. Her father was the managing editor of a Fascist newspaper established by Mussolini in Albania during the Italian occupation. Wealthy people.' He rubbed his thumb and index finger together in the Italian gesture signifying 'money, lots of money'. 'But then the country went Communist, they made us change our name, our passports carrying the Savoy royal coat of arms expired and we couldn't renew them because one wasn't allowed to go anywhere near the embassy. It was in the diplomatic district; no ordinary citizen could even walk along the pavements of the area, let alone enter a foreign embassy. Then we had to cope with everyday life, everyday work.' He paused and searched my face, reassuring himself about my understanding and sympathy. 'In short, we became resigned to the situation. And we're still here.'

Rodolfo came closer to me. I can remember his yellowing teeth, his eyes wide with fear, his old-fashioned Italian. 'Don't worry, Doctor Riccardo. You will be out of here before long.

I've ended up in this cell dozens of times. Just because they knew I was not really Albanian, I was always included in any list of suspects. I've been shut up in this cell for days at a time. I know it well, this cell. We're old friends. Cheer up, Doctor Riccardo. You are a foreigner. An Italian. A real Italian, with a valid passport and everything. I am sure that soon you will be released and you'll go home, while I can never leave Albania, not even now when we have a democracy.' I said, trying to sound encouraging, '*Grazie* for your kind words. But now you can regain your citizenship, maybe. You can be free too.'

Rodolfo gave me a sad look. 'They might give me a passport one day, but I no longer want to apply for it. How could I leave my old mother behind? She's got no one left in Italy and she's very old. We lost. Albania won. We shall die her prisoners.'

The day after my interview with the Widow I had met Erkam, a twenty-five-year-old teacher of French with wild eyes and a denim jacket too tight for him. At first he struck me as an intellectual opposed to the Berisha government. But he was probably one of Berisha's policemen recently recruited from the ranks of the Hoxhas' opponents.

One evening we were strolling slowly, like everyone else, round Skanderbeg Square, Albania's 'goldfish-bowl'. The square had once been dominated by a gigantic bronze statue dedicated to the great shark, Enver Hoxha. Until 22 March 1990, when it was demolished, pulled down with the help of cables by the same people who only the previous day had taken their children to lay flowers on its gigantic right foot. Ramiz Alia, Hoxha's chosen successor, had not opposed the destruction. As the new head of state, with the rest of the Eastern bloc collapsing one regime after the other, the former dauphin pretended he never knew the big shark. To avoid the regime's collapse he even introduced reforms. But it was too little, too late. Most people saw him as the Widow's puppet, so Berisha won the elections and Ramiz Alia ended up in prison.

The new plain-clothes policemen keeping the goldfish-bowl under observation looked identical to the old Sigurimi.

As we came abreast of the former history museum at the end of our fifth lap of the square, Erkam explained that the Albanians had never regarded 'Uncle Enver' as an Orwellian Big Brother, but as the Pharaoh Cheops. 'Just like Hoxha, the Pharaoh knew how to wield power even after his death, from the tomb. That is, from the pyramid. Which is why we in Tirana also have our pyramid.'

Known officially as the Enver Hoxha Mausoleum, it was indeed in the shape of a pyramid. The government had built it in the mid-Eighties beside Tirana's main thoroughfare, once Avenue Mussolini, then Avenue Stalin and eventually Avenue of the Martyrs. It was held up as the jewel of Albanian architecture.

The poorest country in Europe had not stinted on the cost. Upon three concentric floors lined with Carrara marble, manuscripts and photographs of Enver had been exhibited together with personal possessions such as his handkerchiefs, shoes and binoculars. Even the bespoke suits Enver bought in Paris in the Thirties. The outfits of a young, privileged man who had chosen exile after graduating from the French Lycée at Gjirokastër, in Albania's Mediterranean south.

A short video repeated *ad infinitum* showed Enver at the pyramid's inauguration, accompanied by Nexhmije in the inevitable polka-dot blouse and her hair in a bun. As always, Nexhmije was following half a step behind him as a sign of respect – even though everyone knew that it was she who issued the orders.

A small shop was selling books. Some were by Hoxha, like the famous *Eurocommunism is Anticommunism* and *Yugoslav Self-Management: Capitalist Theory and Practice,* both of which were required reading in every school in the land until 1990. One book was by Ramiz Alia, written in 1988. Called *Our Enver*, it described Hoxha as '. . . a man gifted with extraordinary physical and intellectual energy', and went on to claim, 'A great psychologist, Hoxha has found a way of penetrating the mind of the people, liberating it from timidity, creating the conditions indispensable for stimulating the thought processes.'

I bought one of the last copies. Some months later the pyramid was closed on the orders of the new Pharaoh.

The Widow did not like the pyramid. She saw that it had been a mistake. During the prison interview she told me that it was not Enver but the people around him who had wanted it. As with the official establishment of an atheist state.

She did not realise that this was exactly how Ismail Kadare, satirising the Albanian government in his spoof historical novel *The Pyramid*, describes the course of events in the royal palace of Cheops. Eventually, the reluctant Cheops – who doesn't want to think about his own death – allows himself to be won over by the high priest Hemiunu, who describes the future pyramid-tomb as 'that pillar that holds power aloft. If it wavers, everything collapses.'

Nexhmije hated the pyramid so much that she lied even about its construction, denying Enver's reluctant approval of its erection. In prison she told me, 'The government built the mausoleum after his death. The cult of personality also started after his death. He had nothing to do with it, nor had I.'

The cult of personality was, of course, already firmly established in the Sixties. By the Eighties, when the building of the pyramid began, it had reached levels of high comedy.

After the fall of Ramiz Alia, Berisha, uneasy about such a cult, decided to turn the mausoleum into a disco. At first his new 'democratic' government did not know what to do with it. To knock it down would have been dangerous, to keep it open impossible. His idea was to entertain the people in the same building that had been used to oppress them. But the pyramid was closed after a couple of years. It proved too expensive to maintain and it was haunted by too many ghosts that prevented it from ever becoming a place for fun.

Monuments had always played a crucial role in the Hoxha regime. In her cell I asked Nexhmije if she was aware that all the statues of her husband and Stalin had been demolished. 'Yes, I know all about it. I also know that the rubbish is no longer collected and that the country is being swamped with cars that any other country would have consigned to the scrap-heap. Stolen vehicles. I know that the factories have closed. That in the villages all the traditions have been destroyed by this so-called democracy. That people no longer work in the fields . . .' But, I said, interrupting her, there is a free press. The Widow looked at me scornfully. 'Albania is on the wrong road, believe me.' And she smiled smugly.

The smile disappeared at the mention of that other – and living – monument, Ismail Kadare. The famous writer fled to Paris a couple of months after Enver's death. Unlike his fellow Albanians, Kadare was privileged enough to have a passport. Once in exile he revealed himself as an ardent opponent. Was he a traitor?

For the first time, the Black Widow hesitated. The sophisticated Kadare had shown the world that Albania was not the uncouth country depicted by its enemies. To dismiss him altogether was too much. She elected for diplomacy. 'I no longer consider him a friend. He has written monstrous things about my husband, despite the fact that we treated him like a brother for twenty years. But he is still a great writer. I cannot deny it.'

The interrogation in Police Station Number One ended the following morning. Rodolfo took his leave sadly. 'Remember me and my mother,' he said, adding, 'It must be very satisfying to be a journalist, reading news from all over the world, knowing who's dead, who's alive, who's giving the orders, who's obeying them, whether war or peace has broken out.' Then he switched to the formal, Fascist mode of address – '*voi*' instead of '*lei*' – in use when he could still think of himself as an Italian living in Tirana. His words were those of a man who has spent too many nights in a prison cell and knows that the truth is seldom recorded in a police report. 'Signor Riccardo, you are lucky.

You can wake up in the morning and learn about everything that's going on. Even if they say there's "nothing new".'

This was his idea of democracy. And since then it has been mine, too. He completed his salutation as if we were parting after an elegant diplomatic reception. 'I will convey your good wishes to my mother, Carolina Comaschi. I shall tell her about you.'

Emerging from Police Station Number One after my release, I found an Italian Embassy official waiting for me in a chauffeur-driven car with its engine running. 'The ambassador wants to see you,' she told me.

The ambassador received me in his study and offered me a cold drink. But the niceties stopped there. He was not pleased with me. In fact he was fuming about an incident that threatened to ruin his relationship with the great new Albanian democracy. 'I was on the telephone all night to the president. Your interview with the Widow has raised a lot of hackles. Eventually I managed to persuade him not to expel you, but in return I had to accept on your behalf that you would leave the country immediately, on the first flight to Rome.'

The same young diplomat who had collected me from the police station drove me first to the Hotel Tirana to collect my case. The Sigurimi had searched my room. My notes had vanished. From there we went straight to the airport. On the way we passed the maximum-security prison. There was a fresh crowd outside in the hot sun, relatives of those arrested the previous night.

The Widow was freed three years later. Shortly before this, Sali Berisha had offered to reduce her sentence by two years to celebrate the founding of the Democratic Party – just like old times – but Nexhmije refused to sign the application. And she wrote to her son saying, 'Don't be angry with me. I need no favours. I could not dishonour Enver.'

Until her last day in prison she was receiving visits from a large number of Albanians from Kosovo. Equipped with their Yugoslav passports, they usually arrived at the border in the middle of the night in order to be in Tirana by dawn. The same evening they returned over the mountain passes, having spent a few quiet minutes in her cell. This was a quasi-devotional experience. To them she was like a living goddess.

Five years in prison had not changed her. Not long after her release she accepted an invitation from abroad. In Brussels, addressing an audience of 'Friends of Albania and companions in our one ideal of Marxist-Leninism', the Widow listed the benefits conferred by the regime: the emancipation of women, the construction of roads and schools, the fight against illiteracy. 'In Albania the working class no longer exists. There are many unemployed, there is a large proletariat, but the working class has disappeared. The forces of obscurantism have destroyed the Socialist system in Albania with barbarous ferocity and have also destroyed our industry and our wealth.'

The old 'idealist' is unrepentant. History, she still believes, is showing that Enver was right. That Marxism was right. That this new regime called democracy is a curse. Now, she repeats, the proud 'eagles' nest' of her days is a devastated chaos of poverty and materialism, submission to foreign interests, crime, drug trafficking and the humiliating mimicry of other cultures. Hidden in a modest house in Tirana, next to the home of her son Ilir, the Widow refuses to go out. 'I don't want to see it. I don't want to see it,' she repeats. And there is no need to specify what.

After an entire life spent insulated from reality, first as absolute monarch housed in the mysterious 'forbidden quarter' of Tirana, then as defiant dissident reading French philosophy in a prison cell, she can only live alone. Far from those proletarians she loved so much.

I returned to Tirana at the tail end of Sali Berisha's regime. The scandal of the infamous pyramid investment scheme was rocking the city. Several picturesque personalities – a sorceress, a retired general, a Kosovar *mafioso* – had persuaded people to part with savings totalling millions of dollars by promising stratospheric rates of interest. The interest would materialise from the ongoing collection of money. Vast sums ended up in the pockets of politicians. The nation was on the verge of its first bankruptcy.

An international firm of auditors had been engaged as a matter of the greatest urgency. A dozen or so smartly dressed thirty-somethings arrived from their branches in London, Vienna and Rome. For months they raked through the records of the sham financial companies behind the pyramids. Because the hotels were full and offered little in the way of privacy, the government had put the auditors into the only building with vacant rooms, telephones and decent furniture: the Hoxhas' former villa, in the forbidden quarter.

The chief auditor met me in his bedroom. His laptop was lying on the unmade bed, his clothes were strewn on the floor. This had once been the room occupied by Enver's son, Ilir. It was a modestly furnished room in Fifties style, its walls hung with garish orange and green Soviet-style paintings showing factory-floor political meetings and peasants working in the fields at the wheel of triumphantly new tractors. A make-believe Albania, untroubled and progressive.

The neighbouring houses, those of the former hierarchs, had been taken over by various international organisations that now had access to Albania for the first time.

A few weeks after my visit the last remaining money-pyramids quietly collapsed. The cash had already been spirited abroad. The marble pyramid stayed closed, too. Dr Sali Berisha was facing defeat. The Adriatic had become a tragic highroad for traffickers in the human cargo of illegal emigrants. Mother Teresa, the pro-Hoxha and pro-Duvalier nun who lived among the lepers of Calcutta, was dead, but her religious order had secured the right to open a branch in Tirana, next door to a Muslim charity. Her former protector Jean-Claude Duvalier was in exile in the South of France. The Albanian Socialist Party – founded by the Hoxhas in 1944 – was about to be returned to power in its moderate, progressive and pro-European reincarnation. I had received a letter from Rodolfo, saying, 'Financially, we struggle on with the greatest difficulty and dream of better days to come. *Historia Magistra Vitae*. The past is our great teacher. My mother Carolina Comaschi sends you her greetings.'

Duvalier

Above his head hung the portrait of Papa Doc – the portrait of Baron Samedi. Clothed in the heavy black tail-suit of graveyards, he peered out at us through the thick lenses of his spectacles with myopic and expressionless eyes. He was rumoured to watch personally the slow death of a Tonton victim. The eyes would not change. Presumably his interest in the death was medical.

from *The Comedians* by Graham Greene

'It's about time that the truth was told about me, about my family and about this famous name that I was born with. Let me start with the story of how I came to power, because that in itself is a story that clears up many of the misconceptions concerning me. So . . . I was nineteen and just an ordinary young man. A student, as we all were. Well . . . almost all. Yes, true, I lived in the National Palace, the great white building with its Palladian columns in the centre of Port-au-Prince. But at nineteen I still slept in the little room I had had as a child, with its single bed, small chest of drawers and not much else. The very room allocated to me when I was seven years old and my family moved into the *Palais* on my father's election to the presidency. Even after I became president myself, I continued to sleep there. I liked it, I needed nothing more. I only abandoned it years later, when I married . . . and wanted to please my wife Michèle, who had rather . . . rather grander ideas. I left my room reluctantly. As a matter of fact, I even assumed power reluctantly.

'I was very fond of Papa. We were very close. He cared a lot about me. He gave me pocket money every week, but I always gave it to the poor. I'm like that, you know, generous and unselfish by nature. I was four and a half when I witnessed the first attempt to overthrow my father: I saw the armed policemen running into the palace and François Duvalier wearing a helmet to protect his head. After I turned thirteen he began to give me books he considered educational: the biographies of Mao, Nasser, Nehru, Chiang Kai-shek, de Gaulle. He wanted me to learn from them. And in the evening, after supper, he talked to me about ancient Rome, about its political system and how important it was to imitate it. Those discourses left a permanent mark on my mind. From then on I was *marqué*.

'Then one day he called me into his study. He was surrounded by his most trusted counsellors. Even before entering the room, I knew something special was in the air. "Tonton," he said. Yes, that's what he called me, "Little One". "Tonton, you must prepare yourself. Soon I won't be here any more, and for the sake of the revolution, you, as my only male heir, must step into my shoes." I replied that I wasn't interested and wasn't ready. He persisted. He said, "Caesar Augustus became emperor at the age of nineteen, remember? Think of the ordinary people, of our people. Do you want all my work to be wasted?" – "No," I said. Then I was allowed to leave. For a while he didn't mention these matters again. Then – *boom* – when the military parade of 18 November 1970 came along, he ordered me to march at the head of the troops. And on 1 January '71, in his Independence Day speech, he hinted at the regime's need for young people at the helm. I felt that the moment was approaching.

'Only a few months later my father died. It was on the evening of 21 April 1971. I shall never forget that night. It seemed as if it would never end. I wasn't sworn in until ten minutes past midnight, because his advisers waited until 22 April to make the announcement. The twenty-second was my father's lucky day. I was nineteen and president-for-life of Haiti. Yes, it's true: until a few months previously the Constitution had stated that the minimum age for becoming head of state was forty, but it had been lowered to twenty after a referendum. I had not yet turned twenty. But the revolution had to be safeguarded.

'During that night I recalled the history books, the ones about de Gaulle and Caesar Augustus. The simple people of Haiti, the black peasants living in poverty, all needed someone to defend them. They needed a new Papa Doc. I had been chosen by Destiny for that role. I, Jean-Claude Duvalier.'

Paris. The Champs-Elysées. Japanese and American tourists stroll along the wide pavements, their eyes fixed on the Arc de Triomphe. I have made an appointment with Véronique Roi to meet in the bar of the Métropole Hotel. It is mid-afternoon. I sit at one of the coffee tables surrounded by imitation-baroque mirrors. Despite the unlikely hour, three Croats in shirtsleeves are wolfing down double helpings of spaghetti. They joke with a group of girls in mini-skirts.

Véronique arrives alone, elegant, stiletto-heeled. Jean-Claude Duvalier's companion is French on her father's side, Italian on her mother's. Her face is beautiful in a Sixties' film-star sort of way. The couple met ten years ago on the French Riviera, when the 'president-for-life' was still patronising expensive restaurants and travelling in a chauffeur-driven Mercedes. His was still a gilded exile, but his marriage to the beautiful Michèle Bennett was losing its lustre.

It all happened around 1990. In Europe the Soviet-bloc regimes were crumbling. In the Balkans Slobodan Milosevic was embarking on ten years of wars and widespread destruction. And the Duvaliers were going through their own, very private conflicts. Michèle – who had held the purse-strings even during their years in Port-au-Prince – was still in charge of the family finances. But she had no control over the family reputation. So with the funds dwindling as the result of excessive spending, and the humiliation increasing as more and more details emerged about the Duvaliers' past, she walked out. She only walked as far as Cannes, however, where she now lives a few scant kilometres from the rented villa she once shared with Jean-Claude. But rumour has it that her new companion, unlike Baby Doc, has an obscure name and a spectacular bank balance.

So in Baby Doc's darkest hour, young Véronique Roi quietly embraced both him and his cause. She was beside him throughout the divorce from Michèle, and even more importantly after it, when the estimated 300 million dollars (the Haiti government claims the sum was nearer 900 million) removed years before from Port-au-Prince seemed to have disappeared.

How this money vanished is still a mystery. Some went to Michèle, who managed the legal process of separation as she had previously managed the Haitian economy, making sure that not a single dollar escaped her. The remaining bank accounts were frozen by British and Swiss courts at the request of the Haitian government. So in 1992 Duvalier was forced to sell his only property, the Château de Théméricourt in the Val d'Oise, and move into a small house in the South of France. At one point he even defaulted on the rent and France Telecom disconnected his phone. In 1994 he was '*impécunieux*'. Penniless. Or at least he was described as such by his most faithful adherents, the Haitian taxi drivers in Paris. Former Tontons Macoute who, when he fell from power, sensibly elected to live abroad.

The situation then worsened rapidly. Reports began to appear in the French press that the government, unhappy about playing host to a disgraced dictator, wanted to be rid of him. Duvalier responded by applying for political asylum. It was refused. Then a committee of Haitian exiles advocating that he be tried for 'crimes against humanity' demanded his expulsion on the grounds that he was a *sans-papiers*, an illegal immigrant like countless others. The French government, increasingly embarrassed by the situation, claimed that they would have complied with the request were it not for the fact that they had 'lost all track' of the former dictator.

Véronique kept her nerve and stayed with him. For several years they had no permanent home, but were forced to live out of suitcases. Under a cloud of disgrace, they rented apartments in Villefranche-sur-Mer, Nice and Grasse. In between, they stayed for months at a time in hotels, registering as Monsieur et Madame Valère. Bookings were made through a company owned by Véronique, the IAR, but bills were not always paid. When this happened help had to come from old Haitian friends such as Frank Pierre of Miami Beach, head of a political organisation with the sinister name of Capois-la-Mort. The same name as a notorious Haitian rebel general who, during the black slaves' uprising that started at the end of the eighteenth century, slaughtered untold numbers of French settlers. The general, hated by the French army, became a hero to his own people because it was in gratitude to people like him that the slaves defeated the mighty Napoleonic armada and proclaimed in 1804 the first black independent republic in human history.

Baby Doc's financial crisis is now over. His legal status has been normalised thanks to an act of indemnity that has also benefited thousands of African immigrants. The bills are being paid. According to some anti-Duvalier groups, a couple of years ago a Swiss bank unfroze a smallish account (of about four million dollars) because the chaotic government in Port-au-Prince, having missed some deadlines, had stopped asking for the return of the money. With the debts paid, the remaining sum, although insufficient for a return to the luxurious lifestyle of the past, at least allows him to draw breath. And to work for the future.

Véronique is the organising brain behind the refurbished image of Baby Doc. She has put order back into his life, from his finances to his friendships, has restored political contacts with the Duvalier supporters in exile, has persuaded him to cut down on his favourite tipple, whisky and Coca-Cola. She has banished the depression that, according to some of his friends, had been threatening his life.

Sitting at the low table in the Métropole, removing papers from her bag and using the first-person plural, Véronique looks and sounds like a successful company executive. 'We're very busy at the moment. One meeting after another.' She smiles reassuringly. 'But don't worry, the president will be here any moment now.'

★   ★   ★

Duvalier arrived in France on the morning of 7 February 1986 on board an American air-force plane. Landing at Grenoble airport, where the temperature was below freezing, he found the prefect waiting for him with a special visa granted by the then premier of France, Laurent Fabius. It authorised him to remain in the country for just one week 'until his future destination is decided'. Fabius was obviously hoping that some troubled African nation, such as Liberia or Zaire, would agree to offer Duvalier asylum in its eagerness to curry favour with the French government. He was wrong.

Accompanying Jean-Claude Duvalier that day was his wife, Michèle Bennett, and his mother, Simone Duvalier. He was dominated by both, intimidated by both, in love with both.

Naturally, there was no love lost between the two women. 'They belonged to different generations. There was . . . friction,' Duvalier now admits, reluctant to blame either and apparently still afraid of both.

It was more than a simple generation gap. The rivalry had been there from the beginning, when Michèle succeeded in having the title of First Lady of the Republic transferred from Simone to herself. Then she set about making major alterations to the National Palace costing seventeen million dollars. Simone responded by building a palatial mausoleum dedicated to Papa Doc, intending one day to be buried there herself.

Simone and Michèle were two opposites. Mama Doc was the illegitimate offspring of a powerful mulatto man and his housemaid. Her skin was fair, but she was one of the people. 'She always lived in the shadow of François Duvalier,' says Baby Doc, who almost always refers to his father respectfully by name and surname. Michèle, on the other hand, was the sophisticated legitimate daughter of another prominent mulatto, Ernest Bennett. 'The only one in my family that I'm afraid of,' he once said, referring to Michèle, 'because she always gets her own way.'

Divorced, with the figure of a model, two children to support and a lowly secretarial job in New York, Michèle returned to

Port-au-Prince at the end of the Seventies with the declared intention of seducing Baby Doc, whose government reforms and relaunching of the economy had given him the status of a miracle-worker among the Haitian community in New York.

Photographs taken at the time show this odd couple dancing on the parquet floor of the National Palace: the tubby, awkward man with an oversized flower in his buttonhole, gazing dreamily at his partner's plunging neckline, and the slender, elegant woman with a rather abstracted expression.

'A divorcée!' snarled Simone Duvalier, who feared the presence of another woman in the palace. In her attempts to talk Jean-Claude out of the marriage, Simone never stopped reminding him that Michèle's ex-husband, Alix Pasquet, came from the family that had tried to topple the newly elected Papa Doc in 1958. But the infatuated Baby Doc was deaf to his mother's arguments.

As her father had foreseen, Michèle lost no time in getting what she wanted. The wedding took place in the cathedral in Port-au-Prince on 27 May 1980. Including the spectacular firework display, it cost three million dollars. Immediately afterwards, Michèle set up the Michèle B. Duvalier Foundation as her personal piggy-bank. She turned Duvalier's relatives out of the palace and replaced them with her own. Her father, Ernest, became one of only twenty-five authorised exporters of Haitian coffee. Unlike the others, he was exempt from excise duty. According to the *Washington Post*, the coffee was only a front, his real business being trafficking in Colombian cocaine, managed through a mysterious private airport. Michèle's brother, Franz, was apparently following a similar path and ended up being arrested for drug-dealing in Puerto Rico.

On the streets of Haiti people were dying from malnutrition and the bullets of Duvalier's henchmen. In the *Palais*, meanwhile, the Duvaliers were living in a fantasy world of unbridled luxury. The US Department of Commerce calculated that 63 per cent of the Haitian government's income during the Eighties was illegally siphoned off by businesses or individuals connected with the ruling clique. One ousted Haitian minister of finance confessed that fifteen million dollars a month were allocated for 'extra-budgetary expenses'. In December 1980, twenty million dollars of the twenty-two million lent to Haiti by the International Monetary Fund were immediately diverted into the Duvaliers' private accounts via Michèle's 'Foundation'.

Apart from her financial wizardry, Michèle had a very astute grasp of public relations. When she invited Mother Teresa of Calcutta to Port-au-Prince to receive donations for her work, Michèle was publicly praised for her 'love for the poor'. Haitian television showed events organised by Michèle to raise funds for a hospital. Tickets cost 500 dollars, and necklaces worth 30,000 dollars would be raffled on these occasions. When she was tired of Port-au-Prince and those she called 'my poor', Michèle went on shopping trips to Paris.

Jean-Claude disliked travelling and had much to keep him busy in the office. One of his priorities was propaganda. Beside the road towards the city of Port Leogan, the Ministry of Information had placed a large poster. It read: 'I should like to stand before the tribunal of history as the person who irreversibly founded democracy in Haiti.' Signed 'Jean-Claude Duvalier, president-for-life'. As if the words 'for life' presented no contradiction to the slogan itself.

The tribunal of history, in point of fact, lost little time in pronouncing its sentence. The *Palais* was threatened with imminent invasion. At Gonaïves, the northern port that had traditionally been the hotbed for rebellion and where former Haitian slaves had declared independence from France in 1804, starving black people took to the streets to enact a funeral of the president, carrying coffins, skeletons and human bones. A 'tombstone' carried the legend 'Jan Clod Min Place Ou' – Jean-Claude, your place is in here. The Tontons Macoute's ferocious repression was no longer sufficient. The voodoo priests and the secret societies – the pillars of the regime – no longer wanted Duvalier. They started to accuse him of having given in to the mulattos.

The regime was finished.

Michèle, wearing a white turban, boarded the plane that was to carry her into exile. She looked as radiant as a film-star. She was the only one to emerge apparently victorious from the catastrophe. Despite the protests of Mama Doc, Michèle had managed to wrest from Jean-Claude his permission for her ex-husband and their children – the Pasquet clan – to accompany them into exile. They arrived at the airport later than expected, at half-past three in the morning, with Jean-Claude, poker-faced, at the wheel of a silver BMW. The Duvaliers' enemies assert that the delay was caused by Michèle, who couldn't resist throwing a champagne party at the last moment as a kind of farewell to their most faithful supporters.

Véronique Roi shakes her head. 'All lies. Jean-Claude has told me all about that night. The government that was to succeed him had to be set up. There were important decisions to be taken, documents to be signed. We have witnesses; no one was throwing a party. That's a lie. Like all the others.'

On the dockside of Port-au-Prince a few days later they were singing a kind of calypso called 'I'm sorry for you'. It ran:

> Michèle Bennett
> I am sorry for you,
> from now on it's on TV
> that you'll see Haiti.

Meanwhile, on the French Riviera, the Duvaliers had rented the first villa that came to hand. Ironically, they found themselves living next door to the writer Graham Greene, author of a celebrated anti-Duvalier satire, *The Comedians*.

Here, in the course of an interview for ABC's *20/20* programme, a heavily made-up Michèle, lounging on a sofa with a long cigarette between her fingers, tells Barbara Walters, 'I don't want to explain how our system worked. It's too complicated . . . Because when you are president and first lady, you are like a mother and father to the people.' Pressed on the disappearance of public money, Michèle replies, 'Perhaps there were some irregularities of accounting. But I don't believe that the money was badly spent.'

Sitting beside her, looking as bewildered as ever, Baby Doc nods in agreement.

Duvalier took the fickle turns of fortune in his stride
Expecting next to nothing out of life.
Till fortune found a girl who fanned a flame he thought
    had died
Whose burning beauty cut him like a knife.
She touched him through the senses that his mind could
    not control
Then smiling stepped aside and watched him fall.
Betrayed by his own body and the hunger in his soul
Duvalier was a dreamer after all.

'Duvalier', a song by Kris Kristofferson

Simone Duvalier is now dead. Michèle has gone. The strong woman who has taken their place is Véronique, more *Duvalieriste* than Duvalier himself. She flutters her long eyelashes and waves her hands with their lacquered nails whenever someone recites the long list of accusations still outstanding against the Duvalier dynasty: the corruptness of the regime throughout its tenure from 1958 to 1986, the violent activities of the Tontons Macoute, the desperate poverty of the country, the absolutism underpinned by the voodoo religion, the megalomania, the responsibility for the deaths of 40,000 people and the exile of one million.

Véronique denies it all repeatedly. 'All lies. No one has ever shown me any proof.' She swears that the current president, the former priest Jean-Bertrand Aristide, is clinically mad and openly corrupt, and that the inhabitants of Port-au-Prince are appealing to Duvalier; she speaks of the Duvalier 'social revolution', quoting old statistics from the Sixties referring to the education of the blacks whose exploitation by the mulatto élite, which had gone on from time immemorial, ended only under the Duvaliers; she mourns the demise of a black middle class 'created for the first time ever by Duvalier'; she describes her journeys to the Bronx district of New York undertaken with the aim of galvanising into action the groups of nostalgic Haitian emigrants.

'I read everywhere that the Human Rights Watch organisation condemned the Duvalier governments, saying it had found proof of grave violations of human rights. It's untrue. Human Rights published its first report on Haiti only in 1985, too late to throw any blame at all on the Duvaliers.' It's a strange excuse, because in 1985 Baby Doc was still in power. Anyway, Véronique prefers not to go into details about the famous report and presses for a new subject.

Duvalier is late. Véronique switches between Italian, French and English with the ease of a diplomat. No, she never knew the Duvaliers when they were in power. No, she has never been to Haiti. 'My life would be in danger,' she says proudly. 'But I've been to the border several times, only metres away from Haitian soil, at the frontier with the Dominican Republic.' This closeness to her adopted homeland must have been miraculous, because she only had to stand there, a few steps away from the Haitian flag, 'to understand the tragic situation into which Haitians have fallen without the Duvaliers'.

'There's this chap, a mulatto businessman, who controls all the oil imports to Haiti. Filthy rich. And why? Because his daughter is Aristide's mistress,' says Véronique, putting down her coffee cup. Then she continues, disgustedly, in Italian. 'Economic control is again in the hands of the mulatto élite. As before.'

When Baby Doc arrives, Véronique stands up. 'Here's the president,' she whispers to me, in case I fail to recognise him. It is a wise precaution, because Jean-Claude Duvalier is no longer the tubby young man with the triple chin and vacant look that appeared in old photographs. He has shed a lot of weight. He has shrunk, is much leaner. The curls are streaked with grey. And he speaks in a shrill whisper. A lament on one string. As if the energy available to his throat were not enough to move the vocal cords.

When the effort seems altogether too great, he raises his eyes to Véronique and she automatically finishes the sentence, completes the explanation for him. Then she moves on to the next subject, speaking always of 'we, us, ours'. It is 'our revolution', 'our government'. Baby Doc leaves her to it and intervenes only when Véronique, describing the details of a family feud, confuses the names of two sisters. 'No, not Nicole but the other one, Marie Denise.'

They could be any normal Parisian couple, if a little exotic. They talk about the two children, eighteen-year-old Nicolas and sixteen-year-old Anya, as any parents would. The children no longer live with Michèle but attend a school in Paris. Jean-Claude tells me that Nicolas has helped him set up his new website. 'Like all children of his age, he's computer-mad,' he says. Jean-Claude and Véronique seem the essence of normality. The things they say sound reasonable, as does their tone of voice. He is dressed in a dark-blue suit with a formal tie. As if he were still a statesman in power. He has always liked to dress elegantly, even though he scandalised his mother Simone when he stopped wearing the black suits favoured by his father.

I ask them how they lived before the Swiss bank account was unfrozen. They look at each other, amused. 'What account?' he asks. 'There is no bank account. People have said the most fantastic things about the Duvalier finances. The truth is that we have a modest income.' Then he lowers his eyes to the ground to show he is annoyed by the question. And Véronique adds, 'We've always had some financial help from Duvalier supporters all over the world, our *partisans*.'

Maybe those who grew rich under the regime. Maybe those who hope that Baby Doc will one day return.

Papa Doc's funeral was held two days after Jean-Claude Duvalier's appointment as president-for-life. It was the twenty-fourth of the month and, by a happy coincidence, the feast-day of Baron Samedi, the voodoo divinity of death, the man in a top hat who haunts cemeteries in his eternal hunger for corpses.

The body lay in state in the National Palace, dressed in Papa Doc's usual black dinner jacket and white bow tie which, by another happy coincidence, was the exact mode of dress adopted by Baron Samedi. In its hand was a red-bound copy of *Mémoires d'un Leader du Tiers Monde* and the *Bréviaire d'une Révolution*, the Duvalier version of Mao's Little Red Book – in the text of which Duvalier had expressed his theory that 'a doctor is sometimes obliged to take one life in order to save another'.

The guard of honour surrounding François Duvalier's catafalque consisted of twenty-two Tontons Macoute and twenty-two soldiers, out of respect for his obsession with the number twenty-two. Duvalier had become president on 22 October 1957. The date he chose to proclaim himself president-for-life was 22 June 1964. Rumour has it that on 22 November 1963 he celebrated the death of John F. Kennedy, his arch-rival, with champagne. As a mark of respect, the Hotel Oloffson, the best hotel in Port-au-Prince and the one that provided Graham Greene with the setting for the tragicomedy of Messrs Smith, Brown and Jones, had no room number twenty-two. After his death, Duvalier lived on in the voodoo Pantheon as a powerful spirit called Loa Os 22.

Jean-Claude and his mother Simone stood beside Papa Doc's coffin. The people had already begun to call Jean-Claude 'Baby Doc'. It was their way of telling him that they believed the spirit of his father lived on in him. His schoolmates at the Lycée Gonzaga in Port-au-Prince had another, less flattering sobriquet for him. They called him 'tête de coco', coconut-head.

Perhaps (parallels with Caesar Augustus notwithstanding) even Papa Doc had his doubts about Jean-Claude. Before his death he took care to name twelve ministers who were to advise him. Above them, and above the heir himself in the unofficial hierarchy of the *Palais*, was Mama Doc, Jean-Claude's rigidly autocratic mother who was Papa Doc's representative on earth. But the highest authority of all was vested in the former president, now transformed into a voodoo deity with power over all mere mortals.

No one could say that François Duvalier skimped on the preparations for his own succession.

'I'm very proud of my name. I'm proud of what my father and I did for Haiti. Under us the country was prosperous. As you see, physically speaking I live here in France. That may seem strange, because France is the very nation Haiti fought against to win its independence. I could have gone to the United States, or to Latin America. I had a choice. It's not true that I was forced to come here. But you see, I don't speak English, or Spanish. That is why I had to choose France. But my heart is in Haiti. I am still the only one who can save the country, which is now reduced to such a miserable state.

'No, I haven't retired. I haven't reached retirement age . . . And I cannot remain indifferent to the misery of my people. As president I did a great deal for Haiti. Today, despite the efforts of the international community, my homeland has never been in a worse plight.

'I miss the contact with that . . . how to describe it? With that provincial world, the world of the rural population, which lies at the centre of Haitian culture. I used to enjoy visiting the Haitian workers in their fields.

'Where voodoo is concerned, I can tell you this: the only reason that country people attend Catholic churches is for the material benefits they hope to get out of them. But they don't believe in the same God as Christians in the West. They believe in voodoo, the traditional religion and culture of my people. A religion that's deeply ingrained in the Haitian soul. The mulattos don't respect it, naturally. But it was the religion that gave the army of insurgents the unity necessary to defeat Napoleon and the French at the beginning of the nineteenth century. Voodoo was the force behind Toussaint L'Ouverture, the leader of the slave rebellion known as the Black Jacobin and who, leading a ragtag army, defeated Napoleon, winning independence for Haiti. The Africans came from many different regions in Africa, they spoke different languages, had different customs. Voodoo was what united them.

'Do I believe in voodoo? Of course. I believe in the values of harmony and solidarity expressed in the religion. Black magic doesn't come into it; voodoo disapproves of it. There are indeed those who practise black magic. But if a *hougan*, a voodoo priest, practises such magic, the gods punish him. Besides, tell him, Véronique, that on many occasions Westerners have sent doctors, scientists, neutral observers to take part in voodoo ceremonies to see if they could find out its secrets. Not one succeeded. Because there is a supernatural element in voodoo that cannot be explained by science.

'The Tontons Macoute? Originally they were the partisans. Is that what you call them in Europe? Yes, partisans. The sons of ordinary people, boys from peasant families who took up arms to defend their own government. Historically they did not have the backing of the Church. No indeed, because the Church was allied with the mulattos, the privileged classes. But they had four-fifths of the population on their side, and that is what counted. The Tontons Macoute were the defenders of the Duvalier social revolution and the national territory. They formed the people's militia that prevented the army, which sided with the mulatto élite, from carrying out coups d'état. They were known as National Security Volunteers.

'So much has been said about the Tontons Macoute. So many lies told to discredit them. But it was they who defended Haiti in 1958 – a year after my father's election – when it was invaded by foreign mercenaries paid by the ex-president Paul Magloire. Yes, the men led by Michèle's father-in-law. Then, after that battle was won, if the people had a problem, they were the ones who solved it. If a family was destitute, the Tontons Macoute gave them money. If a mother needed funds to send her child to school, she turned to them. If a man was unemployed, he turned to them. They acted as mediators in the absence of institutions. I call them . . . artisans of the social revolution.

'Regrets? One: that I was unable to bring about the birth of true democracy in Haiti. They didn't give me enough time. Fifteen years after my departure, Haiti is still not a democracy. Because you can't create a democracy just by pouring in money, foreign aid. You must have a political culture, you need a political class. That was what we were creating.

'A little while ago I sent a message to the nation. It was addressed to the *Duvalieristes* of all nine *départements* and to those abroad. A message of brotherhood and hope. I said: "This difficult time sorely tries our hearts and spirits, but it finds us united in a common feeling of abnegation, prepared to accept the sacrifices demanded by a national rebirth." I appealed to liberty, social justice and tolerance – that is, to the values of Duvalierism. And I said, "I stand as surety for the inevitable changes; I can lead this country to a moral and material transformation. With the help of the *Eternel Tout Puissant,* the almighty and eternal God."'

The *Eternel Tout Puissant* invoked by Duvalier is not necessarily the Almighty God of the Catholic Church. Relations between Port-au-Prince and the Vatican, which is hostile to voodoo and considered to be the instrument of the mulatto élite, have always been stormy. Papa Doc wasted no time before making it clear that the only superior being tolerated by the new and revolutionary Haiti was himself, not the Roman Catholic God. So, at the beginning of his 'reign', even the Lord's Prayer was changed. The new, revolutionary version ran:

Our Doc, who art in the National Palace for life, hallowed be Thy name by present and future generations. Thy will be done in Port-au-Prince as it is in the provinces. Give us this day our new Haiti and forgive not the trespasses of those anti-patriots who daily spit upon our country. Let them succumb to temptation, and under the weight of their venom, deliver them not from evil.

Schools taught the new 'Revolutionary Catechism'. Based on the traditional question-and-answer method of the Catholic catechism, it transformed the Holy Trinity into a sort of Holy Quintet and went like this:

Question: Who are Dessalines, Toussaint, Christophe, Pétion and Estime?

Answer: Dessalines, Toussaint, Christophe, Pétion, and Estime are five distinct heads of state who are substantiated in and form one single president in the person of François Duvalier.

Pope John Paul II visited Haiti in March 1983, only five years after his election. Haiti was high on his list of priorities. Arriving at the François Duvalier International Airport and having kissed the ground three times – giving the voodoo faithful the impression that he was celebrating a magic rite, or even pronouncing a curse – the Pope proceeded to make a speech designed to shock. In front of a big and incredulous crowd, he told Jean-Claude and Michèle Duvalier, 'Yours is a beautiful country, rich in human resources, but Christians cannot be unaware of the injustice, the excessive inequality, the degradation of the quality of life, the misery, the hunger, the fear suffered by the majority of the people.'

'The Pope was not well informed on the situation of the country,' says Duvalier now, adding, 'and anyway, while everybody mentions the speech he made on the day of his arrival, nobody mentions the farewell speech he made on his last day. The tone was completely different. The Pope asked the international community for financial aid for my government.'

But that same year, a botanist and researcher from the University of Harvard, Wade Davis, succeeded in infiltrating

Bizango, the most important Haitian secret society whose name, like many of its rites and beliefs, comes from West Africa. Davis entered the secret voodoo temples affiliated to the Bizango society and discovered that its most important divinity was the president. Photographs of François Duvalier dominated the altars. The Bizango flag was red and black, signifying blood and night. These also happened to be the colours of the new flag chosen for Haiti by Duvalier after his election. The society had emperors and queens, presidents and under-secretaries. It was a mélange of American democracy, French aristocracy and the African tribal system. The trappings included black virgins, hearts pierced with pins, bottles of rum, swords and grave-diggers' spades. Human sacrifices were not uncommon.

The Bizango society's motto was 'Order and respect for the Night'. It could have been the official motto of Haiti: 'Order' was the obligation to obey Papa Doc, while 'Respect for the Night' was a clear reference to the Tontons Macoute's famously nocturnal raids and activities. Duvalier loved what we now call 'sound-bites' and spent a lot of time crafting short sentences that could be easily memorised by his illiterate and voodooist constituency. After being proclaimed president-for-life in June 1964, he pronounced his celebrated self-definition from the balcony of the National Palace. Speaking in the third person, he stated: 'Dr Duvalier is a giant who can eclipse the sun.'

The new Constitution, however, defined him ambiguously as *le souverain,* the sovereign. Papa Doc was dreaming of the day when he could proclaim himself Emperor François I and restore the long-forgotten Haitian monarchy.

In the Métropole, the squeaky voice of the ex-president-for-life is almost drowned by the guffaws of the Croat *mafiosi.* After each sentence he looks at the floor while waiting for Véronique's translation. As if concentrating on the next sentence, rehearsing it, honing it until he is satisfied that its delivery will be as effective as possible.

'Véronique, tell him that before the Duvaliers' time no black man was ever promoted to the rank of officer in the army. It was specifically forbidden.' His voice trembles. 'Tell him that the children of ordinary people were not allowed to become doctors. Apart from just twelve or fifteen a year. But by the time I came to power the number had already risen to 250 a year, thanks to my father. Tell him that.'

Véronique translates but, not entirely satisfied with Duvalier's self-justification, expands it by adding details of names and dates she considers important.

I ask whether, given that Duvalier considered the promotion of the black population so important, it was not paradoxical that he himself should have married a woman from the mulatto middle class?

Véronique smiles. Pleased with the question, she puts it to Duvalier in a different tone of voice, suggesting that for once she does not know the answer.

'Tell him that apart from the . . . shall we say, sentimental reasons, I hoped that my marriage would help to unify Haitians, black and white. That was another facet of the Duvalier social revolution.'

Véronique laughs and takes over again.

'Were the Tontons Macoute never guilty of excesses?' I ask cautiously, hoping to prod the Duvaliers towards a measure of self-criticism.

Véronique replies. 'There were hotheads among them, as there are in any police force,' she says. 'But if the New York police beats someone up or even kills an innocent person, how come the press does not blame the president of the United States? What could we do about it? The VSN, the volunteers of the national security force, were social mediators. In a country without social services, they provided assistance to the people.'

They were benefactors, then. But the 1985 report by the Human Rights Watch had revealed a rather different reality. In the Caserne Dessalines, a gloomy military barracks some fifty metres away from the silken hangings of the National Palace, the Tontons Macoute had practised what the dissident René Théodore called 'political necrophilia'. Torture.

They had terrorised the rural population; wielding machetes, they had driven them from their homes into the shanty towns around Port-au-Prince. To ghettos like Cité Soleil, with no drains, no water, no electricity. Yet for the ex-president they merited the poetic definition of 'artisans of the revolution'.

'With regard to the Macoute,' says Véronique, 'there were elections in Duvalier's Haiti. Democratic elections, something I always like to remember. And the Macoute helped to organise them.' Perhaps she is referring to the referendum of 22 July 1985, when Jean-Claude proposed two amendments to the Constitution: the right of the president-for-life to choose his successor, and the right of parties who declared their loyalty to the regime to receive financial assistance from the state. The referendum passed the amendments with a majority of 99.98 per cent. 'No, I refer to the 1957 elections, when François gave the vote to women for the first time. He emancipated them. Under the Duvaliers, we had the *femme Macoute*, called the *Marie-Jeanne*, the female equivalent of the male volunteers. It was a progressive decision. Women had been traditionally excluded from any public activity.'

At this point Duvalier breaks a long silence. 'Véronique, tell him that this was the female side of François Duvalier's personality.'

Female side? Did he mean feminist? 'No, no, *féminine*,' insists Baby Doc.

Véronique now intervenes, anxious to turn the discussion away from a subject threatening to become dangerous. 'The Duvalier government had its female, as well as its male, defenders. Duvalier was an innovator who was on the side of women.'

'Tell him about Aristide. Tell him that I am his *cauchemare*, his nightmare,' Duvalier says impatiently, with his eyes, as ever, on the ground. He is tired of speaking about the past. It is the future that interests him. A future without the pervading presence of his father's ghost, without the suffocating surveillance of his mother, without the extravagant demands of Michèle. A future that is, at last, his and his alone.

'Oh yes. The president sent me to Canada, to the United States and to the Dominican Republic to set up meetings with his supporters,' says Véronique. 'It was most successful. Duvalier is more popular now than ever before. And he represents Aristide's worst nightmare, his incubus. Aristide is spreading false rumours about our having paid people to come to meetings, with money from previously frozen bank accounts. The fact is that Duvalier is much more popular than Aristide.'

Again Duvalier's reedy voice makes itself heard. 'Tell him about the Vatican.' – 'Of course,' Véronique assents, 'we have read the internal Vatican reports about Aristide. They say that he is mentally sick. We have proof that he was arrested for rape in the Dominican Republic. He has made Haiti into a narco-state, living off the proceeds of cocaine trafficking. The people hate him.'

The soberly dressed, perfectly groomed Jean-Claude shakes himself out of his apathy. 'I've survived several assassination attempts. They tried to assassinate me when I was a child at school, but killed several of my bodyguards instead. So I'm still here. Ready to devote my life again to Haiti.'

But a return to the *Palais* is probably still a long way off. Is it possible, I ask, that in the meantime he has developed no hobby, engaged in no profession, no business? He was, after all, only thirty-five when he left Haiti. Duvalier thinks for a moment, then smiles. 'There is a subject in which I take a certain interest,' he says. 'What's that?' I ask. 'Solar energy. Yes, solar energy.' Duvalier smiles, looking more relaxed than before. 'My dream is to use the sun to revive Haiti's economy. I love the sun.' And he ends with a rare laugh. 'All of us in Haiti love the sun.'

It could be a mere coincidence, but the sun has an important role in voodoo. Its representative on earth, *Papa Legba*, as they call him, is the little old man who watches over gateways and crossroads, opens the doors of the world to the light of the sun and the spiritual power of the gods. Every ceremony opens by invoking his name.

The Bronx. Old houses made of wood from which the paint has long since flaked away. Soviet-style blocks of flats. Dirt everywhere. Groups of children sitting on the pavements. Smell of *poulet rôti*, chicken cooked in the traditional Haitian way. Manhattan is just across the Hudson River, but might as well be on another planet. This is where all the Haitian exiles converge, pro-Duvaliers and anti-Duvaliers, Tontons Macoute and their victims, Marxist intellectuals and voodoo priests. All meet up in the Bronx. Or in Queens. The poorest go to Brooklyn, the richest to Cambria Heights. And they re-create the old wars, the old divisions.

Queens is the hiding-place of the famous Emmanuel 'Toto' Constant, ex-informer to the CIA and former charismatic leader of FRAPH, the death-squad organisation that terrorised the population of Haiti until 1994 on behalf of the mulatto generals who had seized power after Duvalier. Sentenced to long-term imprisonment for a famous massacre in 1994 (which also occurred in the city of Gonaïves), Toto Constant is now eligible for extradition. The Gonaïves killings forced the Clinton administration to revise its Haiti policy and led, a few months later, to the American invasion of the country, the second military intervention after a similar one in 1915. But now the American government seems to be in no hurry to extradite Constant.

Constant is friendly with Franz Bataille, physician and devoted supporter of Baby Doc. Together they organise special *Duvalieriste* evenings, where supporters rent nightclubs in Brooklyn or Long Island, fill them with the black-and-red flags and are treated to old recorded speeches by the president. Sometimes even live phone-calls from Paris. The talk is of the 'golden years' of Haiti under Duvalier and of the 'current destruction' under Aristide. The more excitable shout, 'Duvalier or death!' Occasionally the activists from some anti-Duvalier movement manage to gatecrash and disrupt the ceremony, causing nocturnal riots and even street fights, before being dispersed by the police.

I have an appointment with the doctor at his home, a bungalow with a verandah piled high with bags of rubbish and bits of discarded furniture. Dr Bataille has gathered some ten visitors, all still loyal to Duvalier. Bataille's father was one of the bodyguards shot defending Baby Doc during the attempted assassination at the Lycée. In gratitude, Baby Doc financed Bataille's medical studies at university. But then (apparently rating his loyalty higher than his medical knowledge), instead of giving him a hospital appointment he made him editor-in-chief of a pro-Duvalier paper.

Bataille is now studying medicine in the United States. He writes articles for the *Haiti Observateur*, a weekly magazine that supports the Haiti political right wing from its base in Brooklyn. But his main activity is working for Chades, the neo-Duvalierist party that he founded with Rahoul Dupervil, an old friend of Baby Doc.

Dupervil had been a young turk in the Duvalier administration. Ambassadorial material, maybe. He was trusted by Jean-Claude because he was witty, educated, abrasive, well travelled. All the qualities that Baby Doc did not possess. So Rahoul had even been one of the chosen few present at the *Palais* the famous night when the Duvaliers fled to France. Like Véronique, he smiles at the idea of the champagne party: 'I wish. No, we were preparing Duvalier's last televised address to the nation. There was only a small group of close friends. Like a family gathering. We were also busy signing documents and making the necessary arrangements for the formal handover of power.'

Over a supper of chicken and rice the conversation keeps returning to the problem of race. 'The mulattos killed Dessalines, together with Toussaint, the other great black hero of Haitian independence. They persecuted voodoo, they persecuted the black churches. They eventually got rid of Duvalier because he appointed blacks to positions of power, allowed them to study, to become priests, doctors, teachers.'

'In those days we were exporting doctors to Zaire, to France, even to the United States,' says Dr Bataille with a rueful smile. Maybe he's thinking about the thick volumes that he has to digest in a foreign land's hostile language – English – before appearing before a panel that will determine his professional future.

Rahoul, a man with an athlete's physique and perfect English, employed as a social worker in Connecticut, reminisces. Like many people in Baby Doc's life, he implies that the president was in charge, but only nominally. His entourage held great power. 'We had even chosen a wife for Jean-Claude. She was better-looking, better-educated, more intelligent than Michèle. But this time he would have his own way. And when she, a mulatto, began to grasp the reins of power, the people rebelled. Duvalier paid dearly for falling in love. The mulattos used the colour of Michèle's skin to claim a return to power and, coincidentally, assert the relative unimportance of Duvalier, now relegated to the role of front-man.' Bataille, a big, broad man who speaks with a marked French accent, nods in agreement. 'Jean-Claude was quite different from how he was described. When we were thirteen I used to play football with him. He was a well-behaved, rather shy boy. Imagine, when he was president, he never smoked in public so as not to set a bad example! Of course, he was young. Perhaps too young. Now he's wiser. Now he would make an excellent president.'

The chicken congeals on our plates. We are talking to pass the time until 1 a.m., 7 a.m. in Paris. At last Bataille announces, 'Now we can call His Excellency.'

The women in the group, plump employees of the banks and post offices of suburban America, stay behind in the sitting room, sprawled on red velvet armchairs listening to Seventies music. We descend like conspirators to the cellars. They are full of bric-a-brac, old refrigerators, tins of paint, broken chairs. On the one and only table there is a white telephone. Dr Bataille reaches into his pocket and produces a paper phone-card like those used by New York's immigrants to phone home without overspending. He dials a long number. The presidential number. Then he smiles and bows to the phone as if Duvalier had entered the room. '*Monsieur le Président, comment allez-vous? Ici Franz.* That guest we told you about is here with us. I believe we can trust him. Now I'll pass you over to him. My respects to Madame Véronique.'

The president speaks so slowly that it sounds as if he is speaking in his sleep. '*Oui, oui.* I . . . have . . . some . . . bad . . . memories . . . from . . . meetings . . . and . . . interviews . . . with . . . journalists . . . who . . . only . . . want . . . to . . . exploit . . . my . . . name . . . But I agree to meet you.'

In the taxi, at two in the morning, the driver gives me a perplexed look. 'Rough place, the Bronx. But I'm not easily scared. I'm from Sierra Leone.' Sierra Leone? I close my Duvalier notebook and tell him that I have recently met Valentine Strasser, the thirty-three-year-old former dictator of the 'Land of Diamonds'. Strasser is in London. He still has the physique of a male model, but is now homeless and lives a hand-to-mouth existence. The driver bursts out laughing. 'Valentine? I was one of his financial advisers. It's a long drive to Manhattan. I'll tell you everything about him. He was a darned sight better than Duvalier, believe me.'

Jean-Claude Duvalier has not yet managed to return to Haiti. He continues to study solar panels in Paris and to claim that he is working 'with abnegation' for the future of Haiti and the resurrection of the nation.

Jean-Bertrand Aristide, the defrocked priest who was president from 1990 to 1991, was re-elected in 2000. But the American government that returned him to power when it invaded Haiti in 1996, claims that the elections were rigged. Aristide is becoming more and more like the despots who preceded him.

Toto Constant – found guilty and sentenced for crimes against humanity – still sells real estate in Queens. Undisturbed.

One of the Haitian generals sentenced with him, Carl

Dorelien, living in Florida and equipped – like the rest of the junta – with a genuine American visa, had a stroke of good luck: he won 3.2 million dollars in the lottery. Then he had a stroke of bad luck: he was arrested and sent back to Haiti.

Michèle Bennett has now disappeared completely into an anonymous jet-setting existence which she screens meticulously from all publicity. In 1997 the government in Haiti, accepting that Baby Doc was too poor to justify any further efforts, tried to freeze the foreign bank accounts in her name.

On his website, which opens with an eerily black page, Baby Doc continues to proclaim that '*A Haïti, nous offrons notre foi et notre courage!*'

Voodoo remains the religion of Haiti. Papa Doc remains one of its deities.

Baby Doc takes the ups and downs of his career philosophically, with detachment. He knows that even if Aristide keeps him out of Haiti and the partisans from the Bronx fail in their efforts to restore him to power, he will get a second chance anyway. The voodoo gods will see to it. His inheritance of his father's mantle, reluctant though he was to assume it, will surely entitle him to a prominent place in the voodoo pantheon. There he may embark on a new career as a divinity.

Mengistu

I remember when this Mariam would come to the Palace as a captain. His mother was a servant at the court. I cannot tell who made it possible for him to graduate from the officers' school. Slender, slight, always tense, but in control of himself – anyway, that was the impression he gave. He knew the structure of the court, he knew who was who, he knew whom to arrest and when in order to prevent the Palace from functioning, to make it lose its power and strength, change it into a useless simulacrum that today stands abandoned and deteriorating.

from *The Emperor* by Ryszard Kapuscinski

'How . . . am . . . I?'

Colonel Mengistu Haile-Mariam repeats the question as if it were an impossibly complex mathematical problem. He weighs it up, allows it to hang in the air for several interminable seconds. He is undecided. Tempted, perhaps, to give me a true answer.

He is looking at the fax I had sent from London a few days earlier. It had taken me months to find his number; no one knew how to trace him. Even the brave journalists from the Zimbabwean opposition papers, prepared to risk anything if it meant embarrassing the regime of President Robert Mugabe, had never tracked him down. Eventually an American colleague who lives in Harare came up with a phone number. I rang and rang, but the phone was never picked up.

Until one day when a man's voice answered. A voice that spoke carefully, in halting English. The man declined to identify himself and spoke of the colonel in the third person, but the voice was the same as this one.

It was the colonel himself, and he was asking me to fax him a letter outlining the questions I wanted to ask.

Now, looking at the letter, Mengistu pretends to reread the questions. He heaves a deep sigh as if to control the cascade of words that might otherwise pour from his lips. 'How am I? I survive. Let's say I'm well enough.'

It seems impossible, but it's true: the soft, hesitant voice, interrupted by sighs, is that of Mengistu. The ruthless revolutionary who destroyed the most ancient kingdom in Africa and sent thousands of his opponents to the firing squad over the course of what he unapologetically called the 'Red Terror Campaign'. The Leninist dictator who deported hundreds of thousands of peasants 'for their own good'. The Red Negus, who made the children of feudal Ethiopia march in the uniforms of Soviet pioneers. The absolute ruler of Ethiopia from February 1977 to May 1991, who starved his country even as he built the most powerful army on the continent of Africa with Russian tanks, missiles and planes worth twelve billion dollars.

It wasn't enough. The guerrillas had neither money nor heavy weapons, but they still defeated him. The burned-out wrecks of Mengistu's tanks now litter Ethiopia, rusty memorials to a pathetic chapter of the Cold War in Africa.

But at the beginning, in the heady days of the revolution, he thought that for him everything was possible – and everything was permitted.

The revolution that brought Mengistu to power was a response to the disastrous famine of 1972.

All of a sudden Haile Selassie, Ethiopia's legendary emperor, the 'Conquering Lion of the Tribe of Judah and Defender of the Orthodox Faith', seemed old and out of touch, indifferent to the suffering of his people. When Mengistu and a group of young army officers arrested the emperor one September day in 1974, it was like a dam bursting: the next manifestation of the African revolution that was sweeping the continent, a revolt against feudalism and for democracy.

In the months that followed, the emperor was placed under house arrest, confined to his palace with his beloved lions. As the drama of the revolution unfolded, the lions came to symbolise the nation's troubled past. When the young members of the military junta came to the palace to arrest one of Selassie's ministers or blue-blooded advisers, they could hear the beasts howling, protesting against their fate. Since the revolution and the collapse of the imperial court, no one had bothered to look after them. The palace stank of their ordure.

Soon the new rulers ran out of candidates for arrest and came to believe that the mere existence of Haile Selassie, regarded by the peasants as a demigod, posed a threat to the Socialist revolution. And so one day in 1975, when Mengistu went to see if the Negus Neghesti, the King of Kings (or the old madman, as he called him), was still alive and found him calmly reading a book in his great walnut bed, his frustration boiled over. And he strangled him.

Or so they say. Mengistu denies it. 'There was no need,' he says wearily. 'Haile Selassie was old, ill and loved by no one. In the past he had had progressive, modern ideas, but the people asked us to get rid of him, so I and my fellow officers did just that. We couldn't have saved him.'

So how did he die? Mengistu dismisses the question with a shrug, intimating that such details are unimportant compared to his revolutionary vision. 'He died a natural death, as far as I know. I can't deny that there were many of my men who would have been glad to kill him with their bare hands to avenge the fathers and brothers they had lost due to him. The doctor looking after him told me nothing about any deterioration in his health, so there was no way I could personally ascertain what happened.'

The emperor was buried in the garden, encased in concrete beneath a latrine. Symbolically, his burial place was just beside Mengistu's office. Maybe the colonel didn't trust the medical report and wanted to keep an eye on the emperor even though he was dead.

A quarter of a century later fate has once again united Haile Selassie the aristocrat and Mengistu the revolutionary; the absolute monarch with a pedigree reaching back to the Bible and the boy from the provinces. Like the emperor's famous lions, the very lions that he used to despise, the colonel lives in an open-air cage, where he prowls like a wounded animal.

Despite the frustration, Mengistu Haile-Mariam is alive and well enough, living in a residential suburb of Harare. There is nothing out of the ordinary about the house where he lives. Surrounded by a green lawn, the house is small, with a low roof like that of an old colonial bungalow, and has clumps of bougainvillaea casting scintillas of colour onto the window panes. It looks unoccupied. But a couple of burly men patrol purposefully outside, day and night, to deter curious passers-by from peeking in. The bodyguards are there to keep the rest of the world out and Mengistu in.

This pretty six-roomed cage is enclosed by another, a cage from which escape would be even more difficult: Zimbabwe.

Mengistu is now sixty-six and his grey hair curls loosely on his head. On a good day, he imagines that he is not imprisoned at all. 'I've not been abandoned,' he says. 'I've still got many important friends in the developing countries, especially Africa. You won't expect me to name names, of course.'

On a bad day – and most of them are bad – he sinks into despair. 'Where could I go? I would be recognised everywhere. I am, after all, Mengistu.'

The colonel arrived in Harare in 1991, a revolutionary toppled by a new revolution. Like Jean-Claude Duvalier five years earlier and countless other strongmen before Baby Doc, Mengistu had been whisked away in an aeroplane hurriedly sent by the American government, which seems to have a knack for efficiently extricating falling dictators. In his case the exercise was masterminded by Herman 'Hank' Cohen, then under-secretary of state and a mediator between the government and the rebels.

At the time the country he was going to, Zimbabwe, seemed to be a dependable dictatorship under the presidency-for-life of Comrade Robert Mugabe. Mengistu settled for a quiet, comfortable but not luxurious life. According to some Zimbabweans, he brought with him three million dollars in cash. A modest sum, maybe because he didn't have time to get his hands on a bigger haul. In Ethiopia he was rumoured to be worth much more, but until the very end the colonel refused to believe that he was going to be toppled and saw no point in planning for exile, preferring to keep himself busy with elaborate but ineffective military counter-offensives.

A decade after his arrival, things have changed in Harare. The colonel no longer frequents the bar of a downtown hotel where he used to sit drinking whisky with the air of a man who would be checking out in a day or two and going home. He changed his habits because Mugabe's men ordered him to lie low. And because he sensed a change of atmosphere in this orderly, very English city: a whiff of the same smell that had permeated Addis Ababa in the turbulent days before his escape.

It is the stink of putrefaction. Zimbabwe is becoming poorer and less stable with each passing month, and rumours of treachery and betrayal abound. There is ominous talk of the president making plans to flee abroad if necessary. People are no longer afraid to speak of things that would have been unthinkable only a short while ago, of new ideas, new leaders, even a new revolution.

Mengistu knows that the developing situation could at the very least force Comrade Mugabe into exile. If that happens, the time will come when his guardians leave him unguarded, when anyone can enter his cage. Even, perhaps, someone sent from Addis Ababa on a revenge mission. He knows that next time the Americans won't be falling over themselves to find him another little house in a quiet corner of the world.

If he learned one thing from his own fall it was that even friends can betray.

★   ★   ★

In November 1999 a restless and angry Mengistu tried to break out of his cage. Using a Zimbabwean diplomatic passport, he flew to Johannesburg and booked himself into the Garden City Clinic for treatment to his diseased heart. But his presence was leaked to the South African press and an international scandal ensued. The Ethiopian government applied to the South Africans for his immediate extradition to Addis Ababa, where he is wanted on charges of crimes against humanity. Charges that would undoubtedly carry the death penalty. Confronted with this danger, Mengistu abandoned his treatment and flew back immediately. Avoiding arrest by a few hours, he returned voluntarily to his cage.

'Ungrateful bastards,' he hisses, his gaze as steely as in the days of the Red Terror. 'I helped and financed the ANC when South Africa was still in the grip of apartheid. I was on their side when they needed me. Now that I need them, they say they can't help. Before I left Harare, they assured me there would be no problems, since I was travelling for humanitarian and health reasons. Yet they were ready to hand me over to Ethiopia.' After a pause, he adds, 'And to think that the men now controlling the government in Pretoria are my ex-comrades in arms, friends, colleagues.'

The 'ex-comrades in arms' who came to power in Africa in the Seventies and Eighties are bound, like the members of any family, by complex ties of solidarity and rivalry. On the subject of Mandela, a leader revered even by his one-time enemies, Mengistu will only say, 'When he was in prison I admired him for his moral strength.' But even this encomium is quickly amended: 'Of his period in power I can see few results. Apartheid no longer exists, at least to all appearances, but no one understands what the new government in South Africa is doing.'

Mengistu has nothing but praise for his host, Comrade Mugabe. Despite the pressure brought to bear on him from a thousand different sources, Mugabe still refuses to extradite Mengistu. He considers him a hero and constantly repeats,

'He has helped in every war of liberation across the continent.'

This is not simply gratitude. There is a political purpose behind Mugabe's unstinting solidarity with the Red Negus. It is a rebuke to Nelson Mandela and a warning to Thabo Mbeki, Mandela's successor, that the heroes of Africa's liberation struggle intend to stand by each other, especially in times of trial. See, Mugabe is saying, I have stuck by our comrade, Mengistu, so don't you dare abandon me now that I'm in trouble. Remember the Seventies, remember the military training that I gave you, remember my hospitality.

The colonel is useful to Mugabe in another way as well. When Western journalists reproach him for harbouring a tyrant accused of genocide, Mugabe likes to remind them that it was the Americans who brought him to Harare in the first place. The same Americans who are now accusing him of being a despot were very keen to help another despot when this suited them.

In Mengistu's case, Washington even offered to help pay his expenses, but Mugabe refused. 'I told them that I did not need their money, that I could manage alone. Even though I was only a poor African.'

Mengistu is no longer kept informed of these political calculations. Latterly, unlike the early days of his exile, he has been forbidden to try to contact the Big Man. So he writes his memoirs, and he drinks. His sole consolation is the telephone. The Zimbabwean government guarantees political asylum, but more importantly it pays his phone-bills, which amount to thousands of dollars each month. He reciprocates by acting as consultant to Mugabe's secret service, the hated Central Intelligence Office.

Some members of his private bodyguard who fled with him from Ethiopia deserted him and sought refuge in the Canadian Embassy. 'When he was drunk he beat us up,' they complain.

Their desertion has only reinforced Mengistu's conviction

that he is surrounded by traitors. In fact, this is a suspicion that has always tortured him.

As president of Ethiopia, he ruled with the help of a powerful secret service and hundreds of thousands of spies, a system modelled on that of East Germany, one of the countries he most admired and liked to visit most frequently. Now, in exile, he has become even more suspicious. The delicate negotiations that led to my interview lasted eight months. He knows that he risks extradition by speaking to me.

Once the ice has been broken, however, the torrent of words from the Red Negus seems unstoppable. 'I'm a military man, I did what I did only because my country had to be saved from tribalism and feudalism. If I failed, it was only because I was betrayed. The so-called genocide was nothing more than a just war in defence of the revolution and a system from which all have benefited.'

It is certainly true that Mengistu's Ethiopia was an extraordinary experiment in social engineering. Mengistu confiscated the estates belonging to the great landowners and the Ethiopian Orthodox Church, which together accounted for 80 per cent of the fertile land. He abolished the monarchy and proclaimed a 'national democratic revolution', making 'scientific Socialism' the law of the land.

In 1982, when the leader in Moscow was Leonid Brezhnev, in Tirana 'uncle' Enver Hoxha and in Warsaw an austere general with dark glasses named Wojciech Jaruzelski, Mengistu fell helplessly under the spell of Communist Europe and rechristened his country the People's Democratic Republic of Ethiopia, a one-party state whose one party – the Workers' Party of Ethiopia – was led by Secretary-General Mengistu. Official documents were couched in Soviet rhetoric. Government officials discovered 'counter-revolutionaries' in the shanty towns of Addis. Their own regime was 'the dictatorship of the proletariat'. Mengistu attended Eastern Bloc summit meetings. Every May Day the Ethiopian army marched along Addis's main street under the shadow of gigantic portraits of Lenin. The best units even imitated the 'goose-step' of the East German army. In return, Moscow sent thousands of 'military advisers' to repress the revolts of the separatists in Ogaden and Eritrea and repulse attacks from Somalia. Then Fidel's soldiers came: at one time there were more than 18,000 Cubans – more used to tropical climates and guerrilla warfare than the Russians – fighting in Ethiopia.

Mengistu's military junta was known as the Derg (an Amharic word for 'committee'). Initially described as 'provisional', the Derg ruled for nearly two decades.

It started as a moderate, modernising government of young, educated men. It became a bloody military dictatorship. Three years after the revolution of 1974, Mengistu put aside the pretence of a 'collective committee' governing the country and installed himself as the absolute ruler. And launched a campaign called the Red Terror.

It was Ethiopia's darkest hour. When Mengistu's soldiers executed the 'enemies of the people', they refused to hand over the bodies until the relatives of the dead had paid a ransom equivalent to the cost of the bullets used for the execution. Amnesty International puts the number of those killed during the Red Terror in 1977 and 1978 at 500,000.

Despite all this, the ex-dictator is unrepentant. 'I survived nine assassination attempts. The country was in chaos. One social group whose ties with the past were especially strong was attacking the workers who wanted progress. Millions of people came to the capital demanding, "Either you defend us or you give us arms so that we can defend ourselves." It was a battle. All I did was fight it.'

Still, Mengistu can't help but wonder if things could have been different. He's put my fax away now, and he's sitting in his small study. A map of Ethiopia hangs on the wall. 'I knocked at the Americans' door saying, "I'm on your side; our two countries have always been friends; Ethiopia even sent troops to fight beside yours in the Korean War. Now we need your help to rebuild and develop our country."' He pauses. 'They replied that they had their hands full with Vietnam and were not strategically interested in Africa. I knocked at the door of China, and they turned me down. So I went to Moscow, to Leonid Brezhnev. I still have a clear memory of the first time he embraced me at the Kremlin.'

Mengistu falls silent, savouring the scene. On that day the African president sported an astrakhan cap like those he had seen worn by the leaders of the Iron Curtain countries. Moscow was cold, but for the young officer from the far Ethiopian provinces the political climate could not have been warmer.

'I explained the situation, and he replied, "Colonel, with the exception of the atomic bomb, my country is disposed to give you everything you think you need." And that's how it was. The USSR helped us materially, not only with words. From that moment Brezhnev was like a father to me. We met another twelve times, always in the Soviet Union. Each time, before telling him about our problems, I would say, "Comrade Leonid, I am your son, I owe you everything." And I truly felt that Brezhnev was like a father.'

Mengistu's choice took diplomats completely by surprise. Ethiopia's ruling élite had always been educated in the United States and Great Britain. The Italian occupation of Ethiopia had been ended by the Allied victory in the Second World War and Haile Selassie encouraged ties with the nations that had restored him to power. And yet Mengistu doesn't feel betrayed by the Americans. A soldier himself, he understands how the war in Vietnam made it difficult for the Americans to contemplate a new client state. Mengistu reserves his hatred for the man who betrayed both him and Brezhnev: Mikhail Gorbachev.

'I knew him when he was a young member of the Party's Central Committee,' says Mengistu. 'Even before he entered the Politburo.' Mengistu loves pronouncing that word. His English, normally quite hesitant, quickens whenever the subject is the old Soviet hierarchy, which he replicated in his own Ethiopia. 'He seemed a nice enough person, honest, devoted to the cause of Socialism. He was warm and friendly towards me. Then, once he got into power in 1985, he began to talk about *perestroika* and *glasnost*. Eventually I called him from Addis Ababa to arrange an appointment. I needed to know what was going on. I went to Moscow to ask him what those two slogans meant. They were slogans that I didn't understand and, if you ask me, nor did the Soviet people. I said, "Comrade Gorbachev, let's be honest with each other. If there is a change of direction, tell me, so that we can also adjust our direction. Your strength is our strength, your weakness our weakness."'

But Mengistu's eagerness evoked no response from the Soviet leader. Gorbachev wanted to call an end to the Soviet Union's colonial wars. He had given orders for the retreat from Afghanistan, which would be completed by 1990. He also wanted to pull out of the centuries-old and seemingly endless conflict in the Horn of Africa that appeared to be inspired not by ideological disputes but only by territorial squabbles. In other words, he wanted to repudiate Brezhnev's doctrine of 'non-capitalist development' for their former colonies, a policy that had encouraged the spread of Soviet states in all the continents and cost the USSR many resources.

But perhaps Gorbachev did not have the stomach to explain this to the devout Mengistu. Instead, he smiled and said, 'Comrade Mengistu, don't worry. I shall not shift one millimetre from Marxism-Leninism. I am proud of our Socialist achievements and I always will be.'

If Gorbachev's political manoeuvring was tricky, the situation on the ground was also complex. While Moscow was sending arms to the government in Addis Ababa, it had also begun to sell arms to several secessionist groups operating in Ethiopia, the Ogaden and Tigray.

'Years later,' Mengistu recalls in his slow, measured speech, 'when the rebels were advancing on Addis Ababa, I telephoned him to ask for help. And he said, "Stand firm. We will support you. They may criticise you, but you have done enough for Ethiopia to go down in history as a great statesman. You have deserved your place in history for having eliminated the archaic

monarchical system, for having modernised a medieval nation."
Hypocrite! To think they gave him the Nobel Peace Prize! He
sent arms to my enemies and flattered me with words. After
this last conversation, I never phoned him again. I knew he was
lying. A very difficult time was starting: we no longer knew who
were our friends and who our enemies.'

Mengistu is tormented by the memory of those last, humiliating months in power. He maintains that after Moscow had
abandoned him he turned once again to the United States. 'The
president was . . . what was his name? Carter? No, wait, the
one after him. Oh yes, I remember, Ronald Reagan. Reagan
refused to help me,' says Mengistu. To him, Reagan and
Gorbachev were two faces of the same devil and his thoughts
turn again to Moscow. 'Gorbachev and Reagan were involved
in a conspiracy against progress. Gorbachev betrayed the whole
world, not just Mengistu. He destroyed his own country and
the entire international Socialist movement, both Communist
and nationalist. He came to power saying he wanted to fight
the corruption endemic in the old Communist Party of the
Soviet Union, but he didn't really want to improve the system
in order to save it. He came to dismantle it.'

In the summer of 1991 the rebels were advancing steadily
upon Addis Ababa. The Ethiopian air force had run out of
spares for its MiG fighters and could no longer attack the
enemy columns. Shortly before Mengistu's overthrow, the
Italian minister for foreign affairs, Gianni De Michelis, offered
to help, in the name of old friendship and in the name of more
recent business deals between the two countries. 'His secret
negotiations with the enemy guerrillas failed. De Michelis told
me that Italy could not help me,' the colonel recalls.

That's when the Americans stepped in. They couldn't offer
him any military help, but they could offer him a means of
escape. It was for the good of the country. They would send
a plane for him, his family and a few close supporters and take
them to a place of safety.

Mengistu accepted.

*   *   *

Many Ethiopians had fled the Red Terror. It was ten years after the fall of Mengistu before they dared to return. The UN oversaw the repatriation of the last 13,000 refugees in 2001. They had been living in camps in Sudan, Kenya, Djibouti, even Yemen.

In Addis Ababa, Ethiopia's war-crimes trials are proceeding slowly. The government lacks the means, to say nothing of the will, to bring the trial of 100 men accused of leading the Red Terror to a prompt conclusion. There has been the odd death sentence, nothing more. Meanwhile, witnesses are telling their stories. Step-by-step, Ethiopia is learning to make public what was once consigned to private memory.

Gizaw Gebre-Madhin testified against Gesegese Gebr-Mesklel, one of Mengistu's provincial leaders. Gebr-Mesklel killed Gizaw's father, cut off his head, and offered it for auction in an open-air market. 'People who have been [*sic*] in the marketplace that day told me about it,' he said. 'I was told that no one offered to buy my father's head, anyway.' Gizaw said that his father – who owned a small plot – had been accused of being a feudal landlord and an enemy of Mengistu.

One anonymous witness related, 'I lost my father when I was eight years old. They killed him in front of my uncle's house. I will never forget the day when my aunt came to school and took me away. For the next few years, my classmates accused me of being the son of a counter-revolutionary. Later, I saw my father's killers in prison. I have forgiven them, as God has forgiven me. But I can't forget what they did, and I want everyone to know.'

Another witness, who did not wish to be identified, exclaimed, 'What days I remember! I remember the terror, the inhumanity, the horror, the prison, the torture, the men in my cell who died, the men who left there. I remember babies that were born in prison, how their mother's feet were bloody from torture. I remember the hope we felt each morning, when we gathered to pray while our guards plotted another day of hell for us. I remember how fifty illiterate peasants were brought in one miserable afternoon, all crammed in one cell, together with their children ... Oh, I remember what happened in the days of Mengistu all too well. I remember my old friend, General Mwerid Negusse, I remember the people who made it possible for me to be here today and testify. And in the depths of my heart, I remember our emperor, I remember the way life used to be: the beauty, the majesty of my Ethiopia. It is no more.'

Mengistu never succeeded in winning the respect of the Amharic élite in Addis Ababa. But not for lack of trying. While his regime set about destroying the traditional basis of Ethiopian society, Mengistu himself always coveted its approval.

At one point he started a rumour that he was descended from an Ethiopian emperor, even though he in fact came from Kefa, a distant province in the south-west that was only recently, and fitfully, assimilated into Amharic culture. The real aristocrats did not even bother to pretend that they believed him.

Mengistu's family was very poor, and he had joined the military for exactly the same reasons as other African military dictators like Idi Amin and Jean-Bedel Bokassa: to escape hunger and – through wearing a respectable uniform – to find his place in the world. But serious, methodical and uncharismatic Mengistu could never become a flamboyant aristocrat like those he met in the imperial court of Addis Ababa. So he studied the great men of international politics – his 'colleagues', as he still likes to call them. He copied their clothes and their behaviour, he sought their company as often as possible. He felt that he too could become a statesman.

'I've met many foreign leaders,' he exults, still pleased to feel that he has been one of them. 'But the men I most admire and respect are the North Korean leader Kim Il Sung and Cuba's Fidel Castro. They have been very generous. Fidel is deeply patriotic, a true revolutionary and very honest. I don't think the world knows him well. Fidel is very human. Very human. And he has worked miracles in his little island of Cuba, given its lack of resources. I have the greatest respect for him. As for North Korea, it's a wonderful country, it's almost incredible to think what they've done in such a short time. Despite the gloomy image that he had in the international press, Kim Il Sung was the liveliest of men; when we went cruising together on his personal yacht he drank, smoked and told jokes. He was a real friend of Ethiopia and gave me a power station, shipyards and military advisers, asking nothing in return.'

Curiously, one of Mengistu's prime benefactors was Italy. This had more to do with the corrupt byways of Italian politics than with any particular fellow feeling. In the 1980s, Italian government officials showered Ethiopia with money for colossal development projects; officially, this was because Italy – the former colonial power in Ethiopia – felt under a moral obligation to contribute to its development. In reality, the offer was self-interested: some of the money filtered back into the coffers of the Italian political parties, including the ruling Socialist Party.

The colonel recalls 'no irregularities'. 'I shall always be grateful to the Italian prime minister Bettino Craxi for his support for the agricultural project in the valley of Tana Beles. A magnificent, generous gift from Italy.' A 'gift' that helped promote the ongoing collectivisation of Ethiopian agriculture and led to the deportation of hundreds of thousands of peasants to the fertile valleys of the south, where 20,000 hectares were irrigated by newly built Italian-made dams.

In 1991 nearly all these dams were destroyed by the Eritrean and Tigrean rebels during their advance towards Addis Ababa. Enormous amounts of money and much human suffering – the combined price paid by Mengistu to get his dams – were nullified in a matter of hours.

The history of Ethiopia goes back 3,000 years. It has been a Christian nation since approximately AD 350. The royal dynasty claims to descend from Menelik, the love-child of the Queen of Sheba and King Solomon. Ties with Israel, real and imagined, have been very important to Ethiopia over the centuries. In the 1980s and 1990s, with the consent of the Ethiopian government, Israel airlifted thousands of dark-skinned Jews called the Falasha from Addis Ababa to Tel Aviv. The Falasha were the descendants of ancient Jewish tribes who had crossed the Red Sea looking for a new homeland. In 1936, when Mussolini's poorly equipped army finally overran the country, Haile Selassie elected to take refuge not in a foreign capital, but in an ancient Coptic Orthodox monastery in the Holy Land. It was his way of affirming that the cultural roots of the nation were linked to the mystical places of its biblical past.

For 3,000 years Ethiopia has never looked west, towards the African interior, but always east, towards the Red Sea. Still today in Addis Ababa one hears talk of 'Africans' and 'Ethiopians', as if these categories were mutually exclusive.

By an irony of fate, her ambitions have always been thwarted by that most African of disasters: famine. The famine of 1972 – the one that caused the first uprisings against the emperor – claimed somewhere between 100,000 and 250,000 victims. That of 1984 and 1985 nearly a million. Although Mengistu exploited public outrage at the 1972 famine in his original bid for power, his critics suggest that he paid no attention to the famine that occurred on his watch. Haile Selassie and Mengistu were both concentrating on the never-ending war with Eritrea for control of access to the Red Sea.

Mengistu denies any such comparison. 'It is not true that I showed lack of concern in respect of the famines. The whole idea behind the Tana Beles Dam and the resettlement of the rural population was to ensure that such famines never happened again. But let me repeat it again: we were in a war, we had to give priority to fighting and winning it.'

As the conversation continues, Mengistu opens up. He still speaks one word at a time, but occasionally bursts into laughter. His khaki shirt gives him an almost military appearance. Now he is talking about Ethiopia's neighbour and long-standing enemy, Somalia. In 1977, as Mengistu was consolidating his power with the Red Terror campaign, Somalia invaded. Mengistu is diplomatic.

'Yes, Somalia was my enemy, but today I'm sorry for the people of Somalia. They allowed themselves to be divided into cnemy tribes.' He has forgotten that Somalia, unlike most African nations, has no tribal divisions. It is divided by clan loyalties, not ethnicity. But for Mengistu, as for most African leaders of his generation, 'tribalism' is the worst evil of post-colonial Africa. 'Even my country has been hijacked by a minority. It has been divided into tribes. Like the whole of Africa, it is regressing, moving backwards into the past,' he says.

But we are talking about Somalia and Siad Barre, who ruled the country from Mogadishu when Mengistu was ruling in Addis Ababa, are we not? 'Ah, Siad!' Mengistu laughs. 'I knew him well, very well indeed. For a long time he was my worst enemy.' And he laughs again.

I have the impression that every time he mentions a reverse in his life, he is thinking of it as a triumph that only just failed to materialise. The war lost just when the problem of famine had been overcome. The ignominious exile just as he had put his country safely on the road to Socialism. The betrayal by foreign friends just when he had managed to put Ethiopia on the world map. 'I tried to make peace with Siad Barre,' he tells me. 'Together we could have done so much for our respective peoples. But he too was betrayed.'

In January 1991, only a few months before Mengistu's fall, Siad Barre was overthrown by an army coup. The two enemies left the stage at almost the same time and in the same, violent way.

In Europe, after the collapse of the Berlin Wall, the entire Eastern bloc started to crumble. Once his beloved German Democratic Republic – the very model of his own People's Democratic Republic of Ethiopia – was no more, Mengistu's fantasy world of goose-stepping military parades faded. The failure of a coup d'état against his arch-rival Mikhail Gorbachev, by Communist hard-liners who – like Mengistu – hated and feared his reforms, only left the Kremlin as the personal fiefdom of an even more dedicated reformist, Boris Yeltsin.

Another traitor. Another betrayal.

At the same time as Mengistu fled Addis Ababa, one of the last bastions of old-fashioned Communism withered away. In Tirana, the widow of Enver Hoxha had to relinquish the power she had held for half a century. She was jailed soon afterwards by the new 'democratic' leaders of Albania.

'I have never been pro-Albania, but I admired their resolute and disciplined philosophy,' the Red Negus says. And adds, shaking his head, 'We have all been betrayed. All of us have been betrayed.'

The colonel stands up. A telephone is ringing in another room, from where the voices of women and children reach my ears. He is anxious to answer the phone, but doesn't want me to see his private sitting room. So he carefully closes the door behind him, leaving me alone in his sparsely decorated study, with just a map of Ethiopia hanging from the wall. I am not to be given any glimpse of his domestic life.

When he comes back, his face is stern. Maybe he has received bad news. Maybe the vultures that are circling around him are getting closer.

Would you ever return to Addis Ababa?

'I love Ethiopia more than my life.'

Do you have any regrets?

'Yes. I built up one of the most powerful armies in Africa, I built up one of the best-organised political parties in the whole world, I defended the territorial integrity of my country like a mother protecting her young, yet it all came to nothing.'

Do you believe in democracy?

'Democracy works in Europe. The traditions in Africa are

different. Look at Ethiopia today. They say they have introduced the multi-party system, but what they have really done is bring back tribalism. Everyone stands by his own tribe or his own religion, not by a party. The same as in the Sudan, Rwanda, Burundi, the Congo, Kenya. Everywhere. The world will see wars in Africa such as have never been seen before. Terrible tribal wars.'

Mengistu's voice rises again. This is a subject that, ten years after his flight from Addis Ababa, still exercises him, still rouses his passion. The world has still not understood that the alternative as it appeared to men like him was chaos, ethnic violence, the disintegration of states.

'As we say in Ethiopia, the world insists on trying to give us fine new shoes. And we have to adapt our feet to these new shoes. But, sometimes, new shoes hurt their feet so much that people throw them away. Do you understand this paradox? Instead of adapting your shoes to fit our feet, you in the West have demanded the opposite. When all's said and done, the sandals I offered would not have been thrown away.'

Months after talking to the Red Negus, I heard a rumour. Mengistu had taken off again, had escaped his gilded cage.

The little house in Harare was empty. They say he went with his wife and twenty-year-old son Andenet, a student at the University of Harare, and his two daughters. Travelling light.

In downtown Harare there were protests against Mugabe almost every day. Comrade Mugabe had sent troops and money to back Comrade Kabila's government in Congo, and the war was bringing Zimbabwe's economy to its knees. Mugabe started to confiscate farms owned by whites. The protests continued. Shop windows were broken. Mengistu tried to reach Mugabe by phone, but the Great Man refused to take his calls. Someone else in the government told him that he was free to go and suggested Cuba.

When Mengistu first arrived in Zimbabwe, he bought a farm in the countryside; it reminded him of the valley in

Ethiopia where he grew up. Now he said goodbye to his adopted homeland. At the airport of a European capital his new protectors awaited him. They were dressed all alike, with black caps, and their manners were brusque. They told him that they would be touching down in Peking.

For a while it was rumoured that the colonel was in Pyongyang, North Korea. The city was cold, and he was living in a flat in a diplomatic neighbourhood. Another cage. The man in power was the son of his old drinking friend, Kim. Out of respect for his father, Kim *fils* would never betray Mengistu.

One month later the colonel resurfaced. Perhaps he never went away, or perhaps Pyongyang was not to his taste. In any case, he now possesses a new ranch-style house at No. 2 Cowie Road, in the Tynwald district of Harare. Tynwald is where Harare's well-heeled professionals live. He has also purchased – apparently with cash – the house at No. 3 Leicester Road, in the elegant surroundings of Emerald Hill. Total value: 150,000 dollars. All registered in the name of young Andenet, the science undergraduate.

It is a buyer's market. The white farmers still hanging on to their land say so at their syndicate meetings. A general exodus from Harare is under way and it is an ideal time to invest.

And so, in a gentrified suburb of Harare, the boy from the provinces has finally joined the upper classes. He is a landowner.

Shuttling between two well-appointed cages, Mengistu has become an aristocrat at last.

Milosevic

That wild beast, which lives in man and does not dare to show itself until the barriers of law and custom have been removed, was now set free. The signal was given, the barriers were down. As has so often happened in the history of man, permission was tacitly granted for acts of violence and plunder, even for murder, if they were carried out in the name of higher interests and against a limited number of men of a particular type and belief.

from *The Bridge over the Drina* by Ivo Andric

The villa was empty and cavernous. The blinds all lowered, the wrought-iron gate secured with a heavy chain. The garden looked unkempt, with grass invading the gravel. On a narrow unpaved path to the side of the house, a youth with a military haircut sat in a hut like a sentry-box, absorbed in a porn comic. He answered all our questions with a shrug, claiming not even to know who Professor Markovic was.

'Are you sure it's the right address?' I asked my interpreter, Maja. 'To me the house looks uninhabited.' I was still hoping it was a mistake. I wanted her to tell me that we had come to the wrong house.

She answered with a crisp, 'Absolutely sure.' But conscientious as always, she consulted her notebook. 'Yes, the address is correct. I'm sorry, Riccardo. I'm really sorry.'

It was the beginning of September. Belgrade was all sunshine and gaiety, with the girls in mini-skirts and the toddlers' faces smeared with ice cream. The favourite area for a promenade, the Kneza Mihaila, was crowded from seven o'clock in the morning until midnight. A catwalk on which the whole city was displaying itself, flaunting its thighs and smiles, its breasts and Valentino sunglasses, in an explosion of vitality to mark the end of ten years of war and madness. The JUL headquarters, by contrast, was steeped in gloom in an avenue far from the Kneza Mihaila. It looked impenetrable.

The appointment with Mira Markovic had failed even before it happened. Perhaps it had been postponed. Or cancelled. Perhaps the professor was offended because, in our exchange of faxes and emails, I had on a couple of occasions addressed her as 'Mrs Milosevic' rather than with her preferred title of 'Doctor and Professor Mira Markovic'.

It was a strange mode of address, simultaneously modest and ostentatious. I was aware that she dislikes using the much more famous name of her husband, Slobodan Milosevic. She claims this is because she wants to be treated like 'any other professor'. In reality she likes to emphasise that he identifies himself with her and not the other way round. Regarding her first name, she changed it herself from Mirjana to Mira in memory of her mother, a philosophy student who died in mysterious circumstances at the age of twenty-four at the end of the Second World War. As for the title of professor, that relates to her advancement from lecturer to incumbent of the chair of sociology at the University of Belgrade. A suspect advancement, the rumour being that she was shown favouritism because of her position as first lady of Yugoslavia. As for the doctor part of the title, this is an academic, not medical qualification, gained through a Ph.D. in sociology of which she is immensely proud and which she allows no one to forget.

I still clung to the hope that the address we had for the professor doctor was wrong. 'This house,' I argued, 'is too grand to be the headquarters of JUL, Yugoslavenska Levica (Yugoslavian Left). The party only got a handful of deputies elected last time round, right? And its leaders are all discredited or in prison, right? It must be the wrong house.' Maja looked at me with an expression that clearly said, 'You should know by now that here in Yugoslavia everything connected with Mira

Markovic is big and gloomy. And, frequently, empty.'

Yes, it was the right address.

At a certain point Maja produced two mobile phones from her handbag and proceeded to use them both at the same time. The phone of Dragana Kuzumanovic, the professor's spokeswoman, was switched off. So Maja said she would try her secret phone. Everyone in post-Milosevic Yugoslavia seems to have at least two mobile phones, one for general consumption, one 'classified'. The usefulness of the latter is unclear because just as many people have access to that as to the other number. But in this instance even the second phone was switched off.

The guard was no help. 'No, I haven't seen a soul today,' he insisted, shrugging his shoulders.

'But that's odd, because we have an appointment with the professor. It was arranged a month ago and confirmed yesterday. Perhaps members of her staff could be inside the house.'

He shrugged his shoulders again. 'The car park's empty, too,' he said, pointing towards the courtyard at the back of the house where the blue Mercedes belonging to the professor doctor was normally parked.

Seated again in a taxi, the familiar yellow Lada reeking of cigarettes and sweat, Maja tried to console me by recounting the history of the house which, after the fall of Milosevic, had figured prominently in Belgrade press reports. A story typical of Yugoslavia in the Nineties.

Before the Second World War the house belonged to a textile baron. Then Marshal Tito – who despite being an old communist partisan was susceptible to its upper-class style – nationalised it and assigned it to a state-owned trading company. In 1994 one Nenad Djordjevic, a former agent of the Communist secret police and a friend of Milosevic, bought it from the state for two million dollars. To do this he had to borrow the money from Beobanka. In other words, from the government. In other words from Slobodan Milosevic, who had particularly close ties with the bank, having been its president before entering politics.

After only one year Djordjevic sold the villa to JUL, recently founded by Milosevic's wife, Professor Markovic to be precise. She was considered the real ideologue of the Socialist (formerly Communist) party led by her husband, but for motives that have never been fully explained had decided to enter politics with her own party, though this was closely allied to that of her husband. By an interesting coincidence, Djordjevic had been appointed vice-president of this very party, the JUL. So when he sold the villa he generously offered his party colleagues a discount of 50 per cent, asking not two million for the property but only one. The condition was that JUL should assume the whole of his debt with the Beobanka.

The net result of the transaction was that Djordjevic came out of it with a profit of one million dollars. The Beobanka, on the other hand, emerged with a bad debt of two million that it would have to write off. The state-owned import-export company which had sold the property in 1994 was duly paid the two million loaned by the Beobanka, but no one knows where the money went. Belgrade newspapers have reported that the company was, in fact, run by friends of Milosevic who used it as a private source of funds.

The history of Villa JUL, however, was still far from over. Shortly after selling the place, Djordjevic mysteriously ended his friendship with the professor. She got her revenge in 1997 by sending him to prison after accusing him of having stolen ten million dollars from the Serb public health service, of which he had been made a senior manager. Later that year a bomb exploded in the house, explained by Professor Markovic as 'the work of the enemy group which is determined to spread fear in the country', without specifying to what she was referring. But everyone in Belgrade knew that the bomb and all the circumstances surrounding the house had little to do with politics and a great deal to do with money – the only ideology of the clique surrounding the Milosevic couple.

'Yes, an interesting story. But what are we going to do about the interview?' I protested in the yellow taxi.

'I'm sure Markovic will see us tomorrow,' Maja replied.

For three days running we were glued to her mobile phones. Waiting for them to ring, like the relatives of a kidnap victim. Every now and then Dragana called us, moved to compassion by the startling number of messages she was finding on both her answerphones. She was, she said, still optimistic. The interview would take place, the professor had given her word. But as the hours went by the situation became ever more mysterious. We had not even been able to find out why the appointment at the house had not been kept. So we took the initiative and went to the Milosevic house in Dedinje, the hillside preserve of Serb millionaires. It was a miniature paradise in the depths of the forest, with country lanes and electrically operated gates. A man armed with a revolver gestured to us to keep moving.

At last Dragana called. 'I'm in a car with Professor Dr Markovic,' she announced. 'We had to go somewhere. No, we're not in Belgrade. Yes, we know you've been to the residence. But we're on our way to a place I'm not at liberty to identify. Something very important has happened. We've had an emergency.'

Maja murmured, 'If you ask me, they're in the Republika Srpska. Or Montenegro. I hardly think they'll be back before Monday, when you've got your return flight.'

But Dragana, in her deep, harsh voice, repeated, 'Don't worry. We'll be back within twenty-four hours at the outside.'

There were no more phone-calls after that.

Three days later I returned to the United States. Without meeting either the professor or Dragana. Maja saw me off with a glum face, as if she felt personally responsible for the fiasco. 'I'm so sorry, so sorry . . .' she repeated over and over again.

After my return to Atlanta, Maja told me that according to the Yugoslav press, Marko Milosevic, Slobodan's son, who had fled to the steppes of Kazakhstan after a close call with a lynch-mob in Serbia, had come back to see the wife and children left behind with his mother in Belgrade. But he had not dared go near the city where, until recently, he had been the most powerful and most feared man after his father. He had opted instead for a corner of the Republika Srpska, the autonomous Serb enclave of Bosnia-Hercegovina, where he could enjoy the protection of the regime's hard-liners, the same people who continue to hide Radovan Karadzic, Ratko Mladic and many other Serbs on the list of those most wanted for war crimes and crimes against humanity.

As a consolation prize, I could always claim that Professor Dr Markovic had dumped me to meet the son who, in the days when he was terrorising Belgrade, she used to call 'my poor, sweet puppy'.

I returned to Belgrade one month later, in October. The professor had renewed her promise. 'She is ready to receive you,' Dragana assured me.

Outside the JUL headquarters the sunshine was paler, but the windows were still shuttered and the garden still unkempt. This time, however, the Mercedes was parked in the courtyard. And the guard with the crew-cut was less surly. After asking a few questions he said, 'Okay, you can go ahead. They're inside.'

Dragana was waiting for us in a huge, ballroom-like entrance hall dominated by a marble staircase. It had probably been built in the Thirties by the textile baron to impress his best customers.

The house, empty and echoing, had the atmosphere of a haunted castle. Dragana proved to be a handsome woman dressed – naturally – in black. Another Morticia Addams. She wore high heels and had the high cheekbones of many Serbian women. Hair as jet-black as the professor's. Perhaps to show solidarity: I had heard that she was one of the few woman friends who had remained loyal to her.

The small sitting room to which she led us was furnished with electric-blue sofas, red tables and white curtains. The colours of Yugoslavia and JUL. Surrounded by so much vibrant colour, Dragana looked even blacker and paler.

Eventually the professor arrived. We heard her come down the staircase, her high heels tapping a regular tic-toc tic-toc on the marble. Her expression was timid, almost fearful. She looked tired. She sat down on one of the electric-blue sofas without so much as a glance in my direction. Dragana handed her an envelope containing several tickets for a flight with JAT, the Yugoslav airline. The professor opened them, checked them and, without a word, slipped them into the Fendi handbag she held clasped to her chest. Then, still without speaking, she started to examine her nails, painted pale pink like those of a young girl, with an expression sometimes sardonic, sometimes abstracted.

Her hair was styled in the way familiar to millions through her pictures: jet-black and bouffant. Like a wig, with a bulbous fringe falling exactly halfway down her forehead. Probably the result of long afternoons spent with her favourite hairdresser on the ground floor of a big hotel in Belgrade. At the same hair-and-beauty salon to which, before the fall of Milosevic, the inevitable Beobanka had coincidentally loaned 225,000 dollars for renovations.

While I was staring, mesmerised, at the hairdo, the professor's mobile phone rang. At last Mira Markovic smiled. It was Slobodan Milosevic, calling from a corridor in the prison at Scheveningen, close to The Hague, where he is authorised to spend twenty-nine dollars a day on phone-calls. About seven minutes' worth of conversation with Belgrade.

Old friends say that ever since the time of their engagement at the University of Belgrade, Mira and Sloba have used a kind of baby-talk with each other, like teenage sweethearts. Even while they were pushing Yugoslavia towards a decade of wars, ruined cities and corpses thrown into mass graves, they chirruped between themselves like the lovebirds on a Valentine card.

The famous little baby-voice now filled the patriotic red, white and blue sitting room of a darkened house. I felt as though I were eavesdropping on an intimate conversation. 'Hello, hello, my darling.' The professor was almost blushing. 'I've got it here, that speech . . . I'll show it to you. And those documents. What are you doing? . . . Yes, I know, I know. . . I think we've got it all sorted out . . . I'm glad we'll be seeing each other soon. Mmm, Monday's timetable is all organised . . . I've got the tickets in my hand. Flying on the usual flight with JAT. Fine, I send you a kiss, 'bye. See you soon.'

She blew the Nokia a kiss. Then she turned to me and, as if to pre-empt a question, said, 'That was my husband. We love each other very much, and that is a well-known fact. The two of us are old-fashioned sentimentalists. In the West you have described us as bloodthirsty dictators. On the contrary, we are sentimentalists. Yes, as I've said before, I still find Slobodan Milosevic very attractive. A fascinating man. A really handsome man, my Sloba.'

Milosevic was forty-five when elected to a post that carried the lengthy title of President of the Praesidium of the Central Committee of the League of Communists of Serbia. That meant he was now the leader of all the Communist parties of the old Yugoslavian federation. The man who chose him for the post was Ivan Stambolic, the recently appointed president of Serbia. Looking for a man he could trust to take over his own seat in the party, Stambolic had immediately thought of Slobodan, his own political protégé. But the choice was only made after months of fighting behind the scenes. Not everyone in the party wanted a banker in the top job. Mira Markovic swung the university faction in his favour. Its vote was decisive.

Until that moment Sloba had seemed set for a hugely successful career in the 'self-management' economy of Socialist Yugoslavia. Three months previously he had still been the efficient, if anonymous, president of the Beogradska Banka, known as the Beobanka, Yugoslavia's leading financial institution.

Mira, however, was well aware that real power lay in political office rather than in business. And so she persuaded him to devote himself full-time to politics, her own obsession. To 'devote himself to the country' which, according to her, was in urgent need of his gifts of intelligence and generosity. So, without too much enthusiasm, Sloba began to woo the party and offer himself for election to minor posts. Until the great leap of 1986.

Even after his election, most party comrades saw him as nothing more than a grey traditionalist, not destined for great things. One year previously, in Moscow, the Communist Party had elected as new general secretary a young member of the Politburo called Mikhail Gorbachev, who had already started to talk about reforms and 'Socialism with a human face'. But the cyclone blowing in from Russia held no attraction for Milosevic, who wanted Yugoslavia to have nothing to do with such dangerous ideas as *perestroika* and *glasnost*.

If Sloba was an unknown entity, Mirjana Markovic came from a family of famous Communist partisans, supporters of Tito. She was an ambitious young woman, passionately in love with the husband towards whom she also felt the pride of the successful talent scout.

When she met him, at a secondary school in Belgrade, Sloba was a boy with few friends, from a modest family background. They immediately became inseparable. She was thirteen, he sixteen. A few years later Sloba's father, who lived apart from his wife in Montenegro, committed suicide. Not many years after that, Milosevic's mother was found dead; she had hanged herself at home. An uncle, too, committed suicide. These were family tragedies that Mira well understood. Sloba attached himself to her ever more morbidly. And she decided to make him into a leader.

Soon after their marriage, something happened that her colleagues at university would remember as significant many years later. Walking down a corridor in the faculty, Mira Milosevic stopped in front of one of the many portraits of Tito, the charismatic leader of Socialist Yugoslavia who had managed to maintain the precarious political balance between Serbs and Croats, the two foremost nationalities of the federation. Looking at it, Mira exclaimed, 'See that portrait? I am convinced that one day my husband, Sloba, will be there in Tito's place.' At the time, no one took any notice of the remark. Mira was a strange girl. Best let her ramble on and dream her dreams.

Otherwise she would get angry. Or, as happened so often, burst into tears.

Politics and political intrigue were in Mira's blood. Her father had been a Communist official, but throughout her childhood he had never spoken to her nor even acknowledged her as his daughter. It was the mother who divided them. A famous partisan, she had been captured by the Nazis. Then she died. But there were different versions in Belgrade of the cause of her death. The official version was that she had been killed by the Nazis. Mira–Mirjana's father gave greater weight to the other version, according to which the heroic partisan from one of the best families had begun to collaborate with the Germans, supplying them with names and addresses. And it was her own colleagues who had killed her in revenge.

The name of Mirjana's mother was Mira. And one day Mirjana – only a little girl, living with her grandparents – announced to her family and friends that henceforth she too would be Mira. It was one way to rescue her mother's memory from the icy silence with which it was surrounded.

In her marriage to Slobodan she orchestrated every move. He never took a decision without discussing it first with her. Friends say that on the rare occasions when they quarrelled, Mira would retire to bed and pretend to be ill for whole days at a time, until he gave in and admitted she was right.

Even the decision to play the card of Serb nationalism rather than that of Socialist ideology had been hers. As a sociologist, Mira thought she understood the issue that lay closest to the heart of every Serb: the centuries-old feeling that history had been unfair to Serbia and that, after so many undeserved defeats, the hour of revenge had come. It was she who inspired the famous speech on the Kosovo Polje or 'Plain of Blackbirds', the cornfields where, almost 600 years earlier, Serbia had fought 'in the name and for the sake of Christianity' against the Ottoman army. And had been tragically defeated.

It was 24 April 1987. Thousands of Serbs were throwing

stones at the visiting representative of the Belgrade government, clamouring for help to put an end to 'Albanian oppression'. Asking, in other words, for the reintegration of Kosovo with Serbia and for an end to the province's autonomy. Milosevic, dispatched by Stambolic to verify the situation on the ground, was not even due to make a speech. But the leader of the League of Communists of Kosovo asked him to address the crowd to calm people down. Sloba's speech, accompanied by a constant clamour of approval from thousands of Serbs, was to become a turning-point in his career. 'No one,' he told them, 'has the right to beat you. You must not abandon your land just because it is difficult to live off it or because you are oppressed and humiliated. I am not advising you to put up with a painful situation. On the contrary, you must change that situation with the help of the other progressive-minded peoples in Serbia and Yugoslavia. This is your home, your country, your garden. You must stay, both for the sake of your ancestors and for that of future generations. Without Kosovo, Yugoslavia will disintegrate. Yugoslavia and Serbia will never relinquish it.'

He was the first Belgrade politician to have the courage to express what the people in the Serbian provinces had been saying for a long time.

From that moment on, whenever Slobodan left Belgrade, he would be surrounded by a crowd of adoring fans. The people asked him to avenge the continual 'humiliation' of noble Serbia on the part of the richer but 'foreign' provinces of Croatia and Slovenia. To avenge the 'genocide' in the Muslim territories of Kosovo and Bosnia of the Serb and Orthodox minorities who, some claimed, were being forcibly assimilated. To stop the 'unjust distribution' of federal funds.

These were the ideas expressed in an anonymous document published in 1986 under the title 'Memorandum of the Serbian Academy of the Arts and Sciences', which had created a big stir and had immediately become the ideological basis of the new Serb nationalism. Acting on Mira's advice, Milosevic adopted the ideas as his own rallying-cry.

Thus the route that would lead him ten years later to become absolute master of 'Small Yugoslavia' (Serbia and Montenegro) and the advocate of Greater Serbia (including the Serbian territories of Bosnia–Hercegovina, Croatia, Macedonia and beyond) had its starting-place at the Plain of Blackbirds. With grim symbolism, the launchpad for the Serbs' future tragedy was a tragedy of the past.

Kosovo was a land where the Serb population had fallen dramatically and the ethnic make-up was now 90 per cent Albanian, thanks to a soaring Albanian birth rate. But power still remained in the hands of the Serbs, who considered Kosovo to be the sacred heart of the motherland. However, there were Kosovars who eyed the nearby mountains of Albania, ruled by the Maoist regime of Enver Hoxha, as their promised land. And dreamed of complete independence from Belgrade.

In the Yugoslav capital in 1986, the year that saw their emergence as the most important couple in the federation, Slobodan Milosevic and Mira Markovic could never have imagined that Kosovo, with its sheep and its farming peasantry, would one day decide their fate. And the Belgrade *Nomenklatura* could not have imagined that the Milosevic couple would become the protagonists of a war that was about to shake the whole Balkan region to its foundations. Ivan Stambolic could not have imagined that only a few months later his protégé would steal his majority by claiming that he was insufficiently nationalistic, and force him to stand down as president of Serbia. Nor did anyone imagine that on the eve of Milosevic's downfall in the winter of 2000, in the city of Belgrade where a string of eminent people were becoming murder victims, Stambolic himself would mysteriously disappear. Probably assassinated.

In the little red, white and blue sitting room Mira Markovic replied to every question in the same way. She listened with her head bowed over her handbag. Then she looked up with what was almost a grimace.

Actually, there were two different grimaces. The first, with eyes cast up to heaven, implied, 'What sort of question is that? You're asking me to comment on a lie, a falsehood!' The second, with pursed lips accompanied by a shrug of the shoulders to indicate indifference and an almost incredulous glance at Kuzumanovic, implied, 'No comment. The matter is of no interest to me. Besides, how could a woman like me – devoted to poetry, music, beauty, flowers – respond to a question so mundane, so banal?'

Then, following the chosen grimace, the professor would reply to the question.

Halfway through our interview the atmosphere thawed slightly. And Milosevic's wife relaxed and began to colour her remarks with sarcasm. This is one of her favourite conversational ploys alongside the baby-talk with her husband, the icy aloofness with her enemies, the sarcastic teasing with others.

'When I go to The Hague to visit my husband, I arrive at the prison on Monday between eleven and twelve o'clock.' Ironic smile. 'This means that I lose nearly the whole morning, because visitors may remain in the prison only between nine a.m. and five p.m. I have to be out of the territory of the European Union, which I am forbidden to enter except for brief authorised periods, on Tuesday morning . . . I usually go with my daughter-in-law Milica, who is second on the list of undesirables. The first is Slobodan; he, it seems, is the European Union's Number One Enemy.' Another bitter little smile. 'Yes, Sloba first, followed by Milica Gajic, my son Marko's wife. The list continues with me, my daughter Marija and Marko. Marko, in fact, is not at all happy with his placing.' Another bitter little smile. 'He keeps asking why on earth Milica is higher up the list than he is. He has always wanted to be first in everything. He has always been a brilliant boy. His disappointment is understandable, don't you think?' Another little smile. 'But there's another matter that disappoints us all. Why ever is little Marko not on the list? That makes no sense.' The professor looks at me with exaggerated consternation. 'What are they thinking of? Marko Milosevic is already more than two and a half years old, before long he will be three. He too is a deadly enemy of the European Union, is he not? He's a Milosevic. A criminal.'

The atrocities of 11 September 2001 were still fresh in all our minds. In the United States, where I was living, the grief and anger were still overwhelming. Everyone knew that we were on the brink of war.

This seemed to please Mira Markovic. At last the whole world would understand the double standards that she and Slobodan referred to when they mentioned 'the crimes of NATO' and 'the hypocrisy of the Americans'.

The professor launched into a monologue.

'I don't see terrorism as a phenomenon linked to a single people, a single country, a single religion. Terrorism is simply a way of waging war. The terrorism current at the moment comes – it would seem – from Islamic groups and is directed at the United States. But Serbia was the first victim of terrorism. Therefore we were the first to fight terrorism and the Islamic extremists. We were the first to stand up to them. What a pity that the leader of this resistance should now be in prison in The Hague, while the leaders who encouraged terrorism in countries other than their own enjoy the support of public opinion at home and throughout the world. That's unjust. But it's also absurd.

'The great powers allow themselves the liberty of having a double standard: one for themselves and another for everyone else. Bill Clinton and his administration backed the terrorism of the Albanian separatists in Kosovo. The Americans were allies of the terrorists, the drugs Mafia, the criminals of Kosovo. The Clinton administration used these terrorists, drug-dealers and criminals as a means of destabilising and destroying Yugoslavia. While the man who defended his own nation is at The Hague, accused of trumped-up, non-existent crimes.

'The Americans have been hit by terrorism and, even though it was terrorism of a less dramatic kind than that which we suffered, have decided to defend themselves with every means at their disposal. That's their right. But then I ask: why could we not defend ourselves with every means at our disposal? Why, when we were trying to defend ourselves against the mujahidin of Kosovo, were we punished by the bombing of our capital? It was sheer hypocrisy. Yes, hypocrisy. The war against terrorism must be fought by everyone with the same weapons. The same criteria should apply to every country and every people. Leaders cannot be treated at one point as heroes and at another as war criminals. And even the terrorists must be treated equally; you can't treat them at one point as criminals and at another as martyrs and liberators. My husband treated everyone in the same way, he did not have double standards.'

The professor fell angrily silent. Then her face suddenly cleared, as if a consoling thought had just occurred to her. 'And then, who is the most dangerous terrorist in the world today?' she asked in a soft voice. 'Nobody knows for sure. Terrorists hide themselves in the most unlikely places. They have access to the most advanced psychological and technological tools. They are protected by sophisticated technology and the communication system. They could well be hiding in a modern city, in an administrative centre. Maybe even a large Western metropolis . . .'

And she laughed her sarcastic laugh.

What does the face of a man who has committed crimes against humanity look like?

Simo Zaric's face is round, good-natured, the face of an honest son of the soil. A little tense, but that is understandable: Simo Zaric has a journey to make. Tomorrow he is due to leave his home town, Bosanski Samac, and board a plane to return to Holland in order to be locked up in the prison in Scheveningen. With Milosevic and fifty or so others.

In the prison housing the Balkan criminals, Simo is known as 'Paganini'. Because he plays the violin like a god and tries to help everyone to get along together, to be in harmony like a small orchestra. Even the prisoners who fought against each other in the war.

The Hague tribunal has allowed him out for a few months. This time allowance has now run out. In Bosanski Samac, Simo is constantly rushing from lunch with one friend to supper with another. But he never stays for the whole meal. Halfway through he rises, makes his excuses and is on his way to the next lunch or supper. 'I've got to say goodbye to everyone. Relatives. Friends. It's exhausting. But I cannot turn anyone down. Luckily, when I'm back in my cell I can rest,' he jokes.

Bosanski Samac is a very ordinary little town. A few streets with the usual kind of suggestively named bars found all over provincial Serbia and Bosnia: Sexy Girl, Paradise, Ferrari Club, Cocktail Kiss. All with their quota of young people in jogging trousers and trainers sipping Turkish coffee for hours on end. A couple of schools in the Habsburg style of architecture. Ancient Audis brought in by emigrants working in Germany. The nearby river marks the border with Croatia.

Until 29 February 1992 Bosanski Samac had a population of 33,000 inhabitants, half of whom were Serbs, one-quarter Croats and one-quarter Muslims – and it was in Yugoslavia. On that day Bosanski Samac became part of the new Republic of Bosnia-Hercegovina. Having declared its secession from Milosevic's Yugoslavia, Bosnia was recognised by the United States and the European Union on 7 April 1992. Bosanski Samac enjoyed just ten days of peace. On 17 April bands of Serb paramilitaries armed with machine-guns, bandannas round their heads and the carefree expressions of boys on a day's hike, occupied the town, proclaiming it a 'Serbian municipality'. Prising it away from Bosnia and putting it under the jurisdiction of the Republika Srpska, the artificially created mono-ethnic state under the leadership of Radovan Karadzic and crucially backed by the Yugoslav federal army. Meaning by Milosevic.

There are still 33,000 people living in Bosanski Samac today. But the Croats number only 100 and the Muslims 300. The others have all gone. One of the survivors, Fatima, is a large, sad woman dressed in purple with black varnish on her fingernails. She is Simo's wife.

A total of 17,000 Croats and Muslims were forced out via 'labour camps' set up on the hills near the river. Of the 17,000, many passed through the 'Mita Trifunovic' elementary school. The Serb militiamen had built torture cells in its classrooms. There they killed, raped and beat anyone guilty of being a Croat or a Muslim.

During that period Paganini was not playing his violin. Instead, he was in uniform and strumming a Kalashnikov. Composing a song called 'ethnic cleansing'.

When he recalls those days, Simo wags his head with the mournful detachment of a man remembering a misfortune that happened far away in some exotic land. 'A dreadful story, my friend. A dreadful story.'

But didn't you see what was happening inside and outside the school?

'Yes, of course I saw things happening that I did not like,' he says. 'I even tried to put a stop to them. But the leaders took no notice of me. And indeed, the paramilitary commanders – all of whom came from outside, common criminals who had put on uniform at the last minute – gave me to understand that if I persisted they would kill me too. It was a regime of fear. This lot were shielded by Radovan Karadzic's party, the SDP. They had political cover, you see? It would have been useless to denounce them to the state authorities. How could Simo Zaric stop Karadzic? Or those who were above Karadzic, Milosevic and his wife? Or that political leader, that very cultured man who is now with us at The Hague, Momcilo Kraijsnik. The guilty ones are the string-pullers, believe me. Those who sat comfortably in their offices giving out orders, not those on the ground.'

Simo is forty-seven. In 'the old days' – when Bosanski Samac was Yugoslavian, not Bosnian – he was a policeman. Then he enrolled in the Yugoslav intelligence corps. A job of secondary importance, low-paid but undemanding. There were not many enemies of the state in those days in Bosanski Samac. He not only has a Muslim wife, but one of his daughters is married to a Croat. His sister, too, is married to a Muslim. Simo laughs merrily. 'You see, now you understand what I was saying. How could I be guilty? I'm a typical man of the former Yugoslavia. My family was typical: it was mixed. I'm happy, I could say proud, to have lived in Tito's Yugoslavia, a marvellous country. A country destroyed by those who began the separation of the various republics, certainly not by us Serbs.'

At The Hague they have established that Simo was a high-ranking officer in a military unit called the 'fourth detachment'. It was part of the Posavina Brigade, a volunteer corps integrated with the new army of the Republika Srpska. The 'fourth detachment' was based in Bosanski Samac. According to the tribunal, its officers and men went from house to house advising the 17,000 Croats and Muslims, 'For your own safety you should leave your homes and go into our isolation camps.' If the 'advice' was refused, force was used.

The illegal displacement of persons is a crime against humanity. But Simo does not feel himself to be a criminal. Only a patriot.

So that we can talk in peace, away from the relatives who want to toast him and the acquaintances and passers-by who want to slap him on the shoulder to show their support, Simo takes me to the office of a friend of his, the manager of Bosanski Samac's textile factory. They were together in the Serbian army during those terrible months. Together in the 'fourth detachment'. Together fighting the Croats. 'A real war against the Fascists.' Croat bullets fired from the other side of the river are still embedded in the factory wall.

Simo has promised to tell me everything. 'It's hard for me, but I'll do it because I truly believe in my innocence. I want the truth, nothing else.' The only condition is that I will first hear his story from the beginning. The story starts at the beginning of the

Second World War, like much of the resentment and hate that convulsed Yugoslavia in the Nineties.

'My elder brother was a well-known partisan. He was killed in a massacre in which eight hundred Serbs died. Massacred at the end of the Second World War by the Ustasha from Croatia.' And he jerks his head towards an invisible point over the river from where the cannons fired at the factory. 'The whole village was devastated. In my family two hundred and forty-two people were killed. When I was born they gave me the name of my famous brother.' The same story could be told by many Serbs in this border region only a few kilometres from Croatia. It is the same story that the survivors of the Serb raids on Bosanski Samac will tell their own children.

Simo drinks a cup of coffee and says, 'Now you know where I come from, I'm ready to tell you everything. What do you want to know?'

I ask him about the atrocities committed by his unit.

'The fourth detachment never killed anyone. It never mounted a raid. We never even went into the town. The outrages were all committed by paramilitaries who came from outside, led by a certain Stevan Todorovic, called Stevo. They also called him Monstrum. We were just ordinary soldiers of the Republika Srpska. Disciplined professionals. We patrolled the borders, we weren't into banditry. We were in barracks. Or on the front line.'

The tribunal, of course, came to a different decision. But, I ask, even if the facts were as you describe them, was it not possible for you, the regular soldiers, to restrain the paramilitaries?

Simo says no, that wasn't possible. It was decidedly *im*possible. He would have wanted to so much, but there was just no way. Monstrum and his men had the situation in hand. They were dangerous.

But how many soldiers were there in the fourth detachment?

'There were five hundred of us,' says Simo.

Armed?

'Yes.'

And how many paramilitaries?

'Thirty.'

Five hundred against thirty. And not one of the 500 dared stand in the way of the thirty led by Stevo-Monstrum, rapist and torturer, leader of the 'security forces' of Serb-controlled Samac.

The Hague tribunal has also discovered that Simo was one of those in charge of the commission 'for the exchange of prisoners'. Meaning the commission that expelled the non-Serbs, handing them over forcibly to the Muslim or Croatian authorities. In exchange, it received the Serb refugees from other regions, the victims of other wars. It assigned them the houses, cars and jobs just abandoned 'voluntarily' by the Croats and Muslims. In other words, the commission redesigned the ethnic composition of Bosanski Samac.

'Oh yes,' says Simo. As if it were possible that such a thing might slip one's memory. But Simo is full of bonhomie. He slaps my shoulder. He laughs. Between bursts of laughter his face darkens and becomes serious. 'It was a crazy situation. A disgrace. A real disgrace, I acknowledge that. But what could I do about it?'

In point of fact, he says, not even the commission was to blame. The commission was a 'technical necessity'.

'The war created a situation in which people, those who weren't Serbs, wanted to leave Bosanski Samac. We helped them.' So these non-Serbs abandoned their homes and all their possessions voluntarily? 'Yes.' And this wasn't the result of intimidation, but of spontaneous decisions? 'Exactly, my friend. Just like that. It was a nasty war.'

With one 'technical necessity' after another, the Serbs of Bosanski Samac succeeded in creating a town that was 'ethnically pure'. The opposite of the multi-ethnic, tolerant Yugoslavia that Simo and the other 'moderates' claim to have loved.

'Everyone made mistakes. Serbs, Croats, Muslims. We all allowed ourselves to be bamboozled by bad leaders.'

When the non-Serbs were expelled from the town, they were taken to 'isolation camps'. Were these prisons? 'No, not exactly,' Simo protests. How were they different? 'A prison's a prison. They were isolated there for their own good. And they were allowed to work.'

I could have hit him, Simo Zaric, the Paganini of Scheveningen. Instead I decide to ask him about the book he wrote in his own defence. The jacket shows a photograph of a demonstration organised in Bosanski Samac in his support before the men from The Hague tribunal came to arrest him. A younger and slimmer Simo, wearing a red tie, is holding a placard. It reads: 'To stand beside your own people even in the worst of times is not a crime'.

I ask him if he regrets that phrase. There can be circumstances in which one's own people behave badly. Is ethnic loyalty more important than moral principles? 'I was trying to say that one should stand beside one's own people even when it is not in one's own interests,' Simo says. For example, if he and the others had left Bosanski Samac, there would have been many more crimes, many more victims. Their presence restrained Monstrum.

Simo is the criminal from next door. He is respected at The Hague because he gave himself up voluntarily on 24 February 1998 to the SFOR, the international contingent assigned to Bosnia. His friends Milan Simic and Miroslav Tadic had given themselves up ten days earlier. Simic's brother was the Serb 'mayor' of Bosanski Samac. Tadic was Zaric's second-in-command in the 'commission for the exchange of prisoners'. Simic, Tadic and Zaric turned themselves in knowing that they were not important enough to qualify for the protection of the Bosnian-Serb armed forces. But they were not sufficiently anonymous to avoid arrest sooner or later. So they played the card of collaboration with the tribunal.

Monstrum is also in prison at The Hague. Same floor, different cell. 'We don't even speak. I despise the man. I play my violin for everyone except him,' says Simo. Another leading figure in Bosanski Samac during those horrendous months, Slobodan Miljkovic, known as 'Lugar', the head of the 'fourth detachment', was mysteriously killed in Bosnia in September 1998.

We emerge from the factory. Simo wants me to meet his son. We find him at his bar, dressed like all the others in jogging trousers and flip-flops. Sitting under cheap parasols imported from Italy. Simo's wife, Fatima, is also there. I ask her if it is true that the atrocities were committed inside the school where no one could see what was going on. And if that was why people knew nothing, guessed nothing. Fatima gets up from the plastic chair. 'In the main street of Bosanski Samac people were beaten and killed every day. In the street. They killed the Muslims for their houses, to give them to the Serbs who had come in from outside. I remember people begging not to be hurt, and still they went on beating and shooting.'

Simo does not contradict her. He bows his head over the table and orders a pear juice.

When Fatima has finished he addresses me, but as if he were speaking to his wife. 'If we had really known everything . . . perhaps a few people would have taken action. But around us the whole of the former Yugoslavia had gone mad. And we were shut up in our barracks.'

Now it is all over. The truth is out. People can no longer say they knew nothing. Some, like Simo, have been arrested. Bosanski Samac is mono-ethnic. The Yugoslavia of Milosevic no longer exists. Sloba is at The Hague, the first head of state ever to be indicted for war crimes and crimes against humanity. Radovan Karadzic is on the run, having stolen millions of dollars from his beloved Republika Srpska. The wire-pullers, in short, can no longer order crimes to be committed. And the good, moderate folk of Bosanski Samac, sipping their interminable coffees at Cocktail Kiss, what are they doing? Are they filled with remorse? Plagued by doubts? No, they vote solidly for the SDP. Karadzic's party. The party that stood for ethnic cleansing. The party that gave political protection to Stevo-Monstrum and all the rest.

'I don't understand them,' says Simo, who is about to return to playing the violin for his select audience of fifty war criminals. Fatima, on the other hand, does understand them. And she gives him a hard look. 'Simo, you know perfectly well why they do it. They are afraid that another party would permit the Muslims and Croats to return to their homes here in Bosanski Samac. They are afraid of being thrown out of their beds. They are attached to their stolen goods, that's all. And so they carry on voting for the criminals.'

In the presence of his wife Simo smiles less, refrains from slapping people on the back, cracks no jokes. 'Yes, they vote for the criminals, the real ones. They vote for the big fish, for Karadzic, for the Milosevic couple. What has happened would never have happened without Milosevic. He is the one to blame.'

For Professor Markovic, however, it was the little people of the world, like Simo Zaric, who 'went too far'.

'I've already explained it so many times over in thousands of pages in my books, and to tell the truth, I'm tired of explaining it. I've been talking and writing about this for more than ten years. But I'll put it briefly. Certain financial, political and military powers in the West had the intention of gaining control of the Balkans. Previously they had found it relatively easy to get control of all the Balkan countries, then they tried to do the same with Yugoslavia. This country proved a hard nut to crack, and it was important because for many years after the Second World War it had achieved a successful equilibrium between East and West. It was the bridge between Socialism and bourgeois society. Its policy was based on high principles and, because of this, it was greatly respected around the world. Western strategists were therefore interested in splitting up this Yugoslavia. A country that was multi-racial and, in my opinion, a model of social cohesion for the European community itself. And that is why I think the Western strategists incited racial hatred and intolerance among the Yugoslav peoples, dragging them into violence and war. They found allies among all the Yugoslav peoples, Croats, Serbs and Muslims. This primitive and stupid nationalism has destroyed us. We are the victims of a hatred that came from beyond our borders.'

And what about the policy of ethnic cleansing encouraged by Slobodan Milosevic and carried out with arms supplied by the Yugoslav army? And the Vukovar massacre? And Srebrenica? And Zenica? And the mass graves?

I have in my hand a book called *The Ten Years' War*. The cover photograph is one of the classic images of Sarajevo under siege. Of ordinary people, clutching shopping bags, running across one of the famous city squares, while from above – from the hills in the background – bullets and shells fired by Serb guns rain down upon them. The professor sees it and takes the book from me. She glances at the cover and asks, 'What does this show? What photograph is this?'

I cannot tell whether she is being serious or ironic. That picture, together with many more like it, stirred the con-science of millions of Europeans at the start of the conflict. It was photographs like this that eventually led to the NATO bombardment of Belgrade. The professor must know that. But as Sloba sought to maintain at The Hague tribunal, 'It was the Serbs who were victimised and made to suffer. We were being killed by the Kosovar terrorists and Croatian Fascists. Yes, the war started in Sarajevo, but because the Muslims killed some Serbs at a Serb wedding, remember? We did not start it.'

But the arms for Karadzic, the weapons used in that tragic siege, did they not come from Belgrade? From Milosevic?

The professor is now irritated. 'Why ask me? I was not the defence minister! I lecture in sociology at the university. How could I possibly know such details?'

These are the details, the 'technical necessities' as Simo Zaric would say, that fuelled ten years of war and massacre. 'What I know, and what all our people know, is that Serbia and Yugoslavia provided material assistance to the Serbs fighting in Bosnia and Croatia. We all did what we could, sending in lorries loaded with food, blankets, medicines, tents, clothes . . . It's logical, I don't know that it's a crime. As for arms, the Serbs of Bosnia and Croatia used the arms left behind by the Yugoslav federal army before the various republics declared independence. But if they are going to investigate who supplied the Serbs with arms, then they should also investigate who was supplying them to the Croats and Muslims. Why do you Westerners never ask yourselves about that? There were three peoples at war, not only one. Why don't they say that Osama Bin Laden armed the Muslims of Kosovo? And why don't they say that this Albanian leader – what's his name? Yes, Ibrahim Rugova – admitted that in 1998 there were Islamic guerrilla training camps in Kosovo? It is not true that innocent people were killed in Kosovo and their bodies taken to Serbia to be hidden. These are all lies, do you understand? The bodies in question were old, a hundred, two hundred years old. We are providing the proofs at The Hague. We have documents, photographs. You are trying to discredit Yugoslavia and Serbia. You keep asking me questions about Radovan Karadzic and Mladic. I don't know what they were doing, what was happening on the field of battle. I was living in Yugoslavia, not in Bosnia or Croatia. Ask those who were there, not us.'

Simo Zaric was one of those who were there, on the front line. He saw the farms burned to evict the people who lived there. The rapes. The confiscations.

'One day Monstrum came to our quarters to inspect us. He had never even done military service, but he had professional officers, real soldiers, lined up obediently in front of him. So the soldiers stood to attention. They were afraid. We were all afraid. You must understand this. We were quaking inside, though we could not show it. Monstrum said, 'If you don't act like true Serbs you'll come to a sticky end.'

But, I ask Simo, if it was all the result of acting under duress, why – when duress is no longer an issue – do the people of

Bosanski Samac continue to support the party that encouraged crime and protected Monstrum?

'I don't know, I don't know. I've answered enough questions, quite enough. I have to go.'

In his heart of hearts, Simo Zaric is not too unhappy about returning to Scheveningen. A new Yugoslavia has been created there, Yugoslavia as it used to be. Serbs, Croats, Muslims, all together. All equal. All guilty. All happy to listen to the same Gypsy-influenced music played by Paganini on his violin.

'I'm an atheist. My whole generation is atheist. But I'm not a Marxist. You Westerners have written that I'm a Marxist. But have you never read my books? I'm a sociologist, solely and simply, not a Marxist sociologist. I teach the same sociology that is taught throughout the world. But I believe in a new kind of Socialism based on the best models, theoretical and practical, of Socialism as we have known it up to now, and of capitalism. Perhaps this society will not be called Socialist, maybe it will have a different name, but no matter. What matters is that in this society people should be happy, live well, have equal rights. As for nationalism, that's another lie about us: we are patriotic, not nationalistic. We have attended university, read books. We are well aware of the difference.'

The professor used to call him 'my sweet puppy'. To everyone else, Marko Milosevic was a kind of gangster. His disco, Madonna – despite its name – had little that was holy about it and was frequented by the whole of the Belgrade Mafia. Madonna was opened in Pozarevac, the little town where Slobodan Milosevic was born. Marko was in business: mostly contraband. But also a theme park, 'Bambyland'. An abortion clinic. A chain of bakeries. The Internet provider Madonna. And there were a lot of favours to friends. Slobodan Milosevic told his son to restrain himself. 'Forget about the abortion clinic,' he shouted down the phone when Marko rang to tell his parents about his latest clever business idea. 'Concentrate on Madonna and make it into a decent business.'

During another phone-call, Milosevic is speaking to his daughter, Marija, owner of a television station (financed by the state). 'Please, it's New Year for everyone. People must be sick of seeing me on television. Leave me and everyone else in peace for one day. God himself is sick of seeing me on television. So am I.'

'But I'm not. Still, I'll do as you say.'

The professor doesn't recall these conversations, taped by the Croatian Intelligence. She tends to forget the fear inspired by the regime among common people and the censorship that was enforced on the press. There was a time when the Belgrade papers and television whipped up hatred by showing pictures of suffering Serbs, and supported Sloba's regime.

She replies, 'You write that we're rich, and we're not. You write that Milosevic was an autocrat, but it's not true. Had he been an autocrat, ninety-five per cent of the media would not have been in the hands of an opposition constantly attacking him.'

Ninety-five per cent.

True. But 95 per cent of the newspapers and television stations were in the pay of Milosevic. It was the other 5 per cent that opposed him, probably paying with their lives.

In Belgrade they call her 'The Red Witch'. When her power was at its peak, Mira had a column in several women's magazines under the title 'Night and Day'. Everyone read it to learn who would be the next victim of a 'mysterious gunfight'. Or who was in favour. Or what mood the Milosevic couple was in.

At times, after the latest in the numberless string of accidents in which her son Marko had written off a Porsche or a Mercedes, Mira would write, with maternal indulgence, 'Marko loves playing with his cars, as he did as a child.' Sometimes she celebrated the songs of the birds in the fields on a spring morning. Or the blooming of the flowers on Serbia's mountains. Frequently she wrote about music.

'I'm Cancer. They say that for Cancerians music is life itself.

I love music that reminds me of certain things, music that's beautiful, cultured, modern ... Everything except classical music. Don't write this down, but I don't like anything that's old. I never visit museums. In the past I did it to please the people living in the city I was visiting with Slobodan Milosevic. But we are more attracted to things that are modern, new.

'I cannot speak for my husband. I really cannot tell if he has made any mistakes. As far as I'm concerned, sometimes – but only sometimes – I think I should perhaps have focused my energies more. University, publicity, science, politics. I've been involved with all these at the same time, and perhaps that is why I haven't been more successful. But then I comfort myself by thinking that all these things complement each other.'

And what about the arrest of Milosevic? Was it a mistake to agree to extradition? 'I don't know, I'd rather not say,' says the professor.

The argument has split the Milosevic clan. The daughter, Marija, was against her father giving himself up. She fired at the police. She is still angry with him and refuses to visit him in The Hague because he rejected her advice: suicide. They say that Marija is addicted to drugs. That after she was arrested for shooting at the police, enough medicines were found in the house to stock a chemist's shop. She lives alone in Montenegro.

And Marko? Where is he living? 'Oh, a long way away,' says Mira Markovic. 'He never wants to live here again. He's been so embittered by everything that's happened . . .' Meaning that he feels some contrition? The question rises spontaneously to my lips, but I dare not ask it. 'Of course he's very young, and perhaps he'll come to feel differently, but for now he's badly hurt and simply cannot believe that the people have treated his father in this way. A father who sacrificed his life, his family and all our lives for the people.'

Dear Zoran,
I have never been so far from you and yet so near. I am

in Southern India, in Madras. I can't be in Belgrade today to say goodbye. To bid farewell to you, the best friend I've had these last fifteen years. But I send you a message that will fly over the mountains and the oceans. And I will never be separated from you.

My first thought was: no more conversations, sharing of ideas, affection, squabbles, hopes. All concentrated into the same time. All that had lasted for years.

I shall miss you until I die. And I wish you could tell me, now that you are about to leave me, that you are not leaving me. Please, look after all of us who are left here, and in exchange I promise that I will look after you. And please don't be cross with me because of those few occasions when I scolded you. You have always been my companion. And besides, I have now forgiven you everything.

You helped everybody, all those who needed it and even those who didn't. It was this that united us.

I shall always be here for Danijela and shall love your children as I loved you.

Adieu,
Mira

It was 24 October 1997. Zoran Todorovic, nicknamed 'Kundak', the thirty-eight-year-old ultra-wealthy head of Beopetrol and general secretary of JUL, had just got out of his black Mercedes and was about to enter the company's head office. Kundak was Mira Markovic's prime ally. Together they had removed the directors of all the state-owned companies in Yugoslavia. They called this the 'anti-bureaucratic revolution'. Then Kundak had thrown himself into the business of buying up newly privatised companies, making use of classified information accessible only to the JUL top brass. Then he returned to politics. A poet who, like Mira, wrote under a pseudonym, Kundak was a close colleague of Slobodan Milosevic, but he was also an embarrassment that many in the Serb Socialist party, including the leader Sloba, would have preferred not to have at their side. That day a man carrying a revolver fitted with a silencer came up to Kundak and killed him with two shots. Mira was in India promoting her latest book. Her faxed letter was read out to all the Yugoslav leaders.

At the funeral, Milosevic burst into tears.

The killer has never been caught.

Eight months previously Vlada Kovacevic had been killed. Known as 'Tref', he was a business partner of Marko Milosevic, founder of the Tref automobile racing company and joint owner with Marko of the Interspeed company. He specialised in contraband cigarettes and duty-free goods and traded in everything that the UN embargo had made hard to come by.

The killer had fired four shots. Marko Milosevic appeared fifteen minutes later beside the body of his friend. In tears.

On 11 April 1997 it was the turn of Radovan Stojicic, nicknamed 'Badza' or sometimes 'Brutus'. He was the deputy minister of the interior. Stojicic was sitting at a table in the Mamma Mia restaurant, enjoying his usual plate of spaghetti. He had spent a lifetime in uniform, first as a police officer, then as co-ordinator of the 'volunteer' paramilitaries sent to fight in Croatia and Bosnia. Stojicic had found a handful of young Serbs, common criminals being sought by Interpol, and had put them in charge of detachments assigned to high-risk missions. One was 'Commander Arkan', the bank robber Zeljko Raznatovic, who had taken a leading part in ferocious raids in eastern Slavonia. Badza provided arms and money. He too commanded a unit, the 'red berets', organised by the Yugoslav minister of the interior and identified by many witnesses as being responsible for atrocities, especially in the Croat Krajina.

Stojicic was killed by seven shots fired at close range by a masked man. A briefcase containing 700,000 German marks was found close to his body. Slobodan, Marko and Marija Milosevic attended his funeral. On this occasion, too, Sloba burst into tears. Another with tears in his eyes was Arkan.

Exactly two years later, on 11 April 1999, a well-known

journalist who had been a personal friend of Mira Markovic was killed as he parked his car. His name was Slavko Curuvija. He was the proprietor of several newspapers, including the daily *Dnevni Telegraf*, one of the few papers that had dared to criticise the regime. The man who had published the photographs of Marko Milosevic with a revolver tucked into his belt. And embarrassing interviews with ex-paramilitaries who revealed details of the links between the political world of Belgrade and the massacres on the battlefronts in Krajina, Slavonia and Bosnia. Slavko Curuvija and Mira Markovic had quarrelled one evening at the Milosevics' home. Voices had been raised. Mira's column 'Night and Day' had hinted that Curuvija was a marked man. Heading more towards night than day. The assassination made a stir abroad. But NATO bombs were falling on Belgrade, and in Yugoslavia no one had time to weep for him. The Milosevic clan did not attend his funeral.

Three years later Commander Arkan, latterly turned businessman, was killed in a Belgrade hotel.

Many others died during those months.

The new Serb minister of the interior, Dusan Mihajlovic, claims that it was the old Yugoslav secret service, the SDB, who killed both Curuvija and the former president, Ivan Stambolic. And perhaps also Arkan. All one-time friends who knew too much.

Professor Markovic still mourns her friend 'Kundak', poet and insider dealer.

'Bosanski Samac wasn't the only place where blood was flowing. We were the prisoners of a situation bigger than ourselves. Perhaps we didn't put up enough resistance. I regret that. But you must go to the big cities, to Belgrade, Pale and Banja Luka, where the leaders were, to find the real proof of guilt.'

Simo Zaric is clutching his suitcase. Tomorrow he will be at the Orange Hotel, as the prison in Scheveningen is called. At Number 32 on a road called Pompstationsweg.

Professor Markovic is also clutching a suitcase. In a little while she too will be setting off for the Orange Hotel.

'My husband will be seen as the hero of all the little people who are the victims of the arrogance of great powers. He'll go down in history as a great freedom fighter. Mass graves? An invention. I'm proud of my people. The only thing I'm not proud about is that the leader of this people has been illegally arrested and extradited thanks to a puppet government funded by the West.' And speaking of The Hague tribunal she repeats the word 'insolent' several times. As if speaking about etiquette. About respectful formalities.

Dragana Kuzumanovic escorts Maja and me to the door of the JUL headquarters. A friend, Ivo, is waiting for us at a *Bierhalle*. He is an opera singer, about thirty years old. Round-faced like the Serbs of mythology and folklore, with a red beard and rosy-apple cheeks.

I tell him about Simo and the professor. Ivo was in uniform, halfway through his military service, when the NATO bombing of Belgrade began. 'Simo is one of the many who believed in the propaganda put out by Milosevic to make us believe that Serbs all over Croatia were being massacred and tortured while the rest of the world couldn't care less. You are one of the many in Europe who believe that it was right to bomb us. To kill civilians. I am one of the many who will never forgive Sloba. But I will never forgive the West, either. You Europeans ought to be in the dock with Sloba at The Hague. But let's have a drink.'

Our beer arrives, with a plate of snacks on skewers. A little string band – violin, viola and guitar – is playing Serb folk songs, full of searing sadness and nostalgic melodies. Ivo sings, moved almost to tears. At the tables nearby, men dressed in black suits and white ties switch off their mobile phones (even the secret ones) and listen to Ivo and the band. Everyone seems to know the words.

This is Belgrade, secular and cosmopolitan. Not Bosanski Samac, poor and inward-looking, caught in the ethnically cleansed Brcko corridor. Ivo has a degree, has travelled abroad, speaks English. When the music stops he winks at me and says,

'The old, great Serbian heart . . . Everything else lies in ruins, but that is still intact. You'll see, one day we'll avenge ourselves.'

Those who passed through the 'Mita Trifunovic' elementary school in Bosanski Samac will never have that opportunity.

General
Manuel Antonio Noriega

2 August 2000
Distinguido Señor Orizio,

Thank you for sending me your book about *Lost White Tribes*. With the help of my dictionaries I am reading this interesting book and today I started the chapter about German slaves in Jamaica.

With reference to your request for an interview in connection with a projected book about certain 'forgotten individuals', once-powerful people who have been blamed for the problems encountered by their respective countries, etc., my response is that I do not consider myself to be a 'forgotten individual', because God, the great Creator of the universe, He who writes straight albeit with occasionally crooked lines, has not yet written the last word on MANUEL A. NORIEGA!

Thank you for your elegant and generous letter/s of June and also for your telephone call to Don Arturo Blanco.

Respetuosamente,
Manuel Antonio Noriega

Acknowledgements

The author and publishers are grateful to the following for permission to reproduce illustrative material:

Amin: Corbis
Bokassa: Corbis
Mengistu: Rex Features
Enver Hoxha: Camera Press
Nexhmije Hoxha: Sciacca/Grazia Neri
Duvalier: Corbis
Jaruzelski: Agence France Presse
Slobodan and Mira Milosevic: Agence France Presse

All efforts to trace holders of copyright material have been made but the publishers will gladly rectify any errors or omissions in future editions. Grateful acknowledgement is made to those listed below for permission to reproduce text:

Nomad by Mary Anne Fitzgerald, permission granted by Penguin Putnam Inc.; *The Bridge Over The Drina* by Ivo Andric, permission granted by HarperCollins Publishers; *The Pyramid* by Ismail Kadare, permission granted by The Random House Group; *The Last King of Scotland* by Giles Foden, permission granted by Faber and Faber; *The Emperor* by Ryszard Kapuscinski, permission granted by Harcourt; *The Comedians* by Graham Greene, permission granted by David Higham Associates.